MOSAIC
WORKSHOP

MOSAIC
WORKSHOP

Emma Biggs & Tessa Hunkin

DAVID & CHARLES

Acknowledgements
Thanks to everyone at the Mosaic Workshop,
Shona Wood, Clare Richardson &
Walter Bernadin.
Thanks Matt, thanks Adam.

Picture Credits
Page 6, top: Fitzwilliam Museum, University of
Cambridge, UK/Bridgeman Art Library,
London/NewYork; Page 6 (bottom):
Villa Romana del Casale, Piazza Armerina, Sicily,
Italy/Bridgeman Art Library, London/New York; Page 7:
Leeds Museums and Galleries (City Art Gallery),
UK/Bridgeman Art Library, London/New York; Page 8:
San Marco, Venice, Italy/Francesco Turio
Bohm/Bridgeman Art Library, London/New york; Page
9: The National Gallery, London; Page 98: San Vitale,
Ravenna, Italy/Bridgeman, London/New York.

A DAVID & CHARLES BOOK

First published in the UK in 1999

Text Copyright © Emma Biggs and Tessa Hunkin

A catalogue record for this book is available from the
British Library

ISBN 0 7153 0852 1

Photographer: Shona Wood
Designer: Sue Michniewicz

Printed in Italy by Garzanti Verga
for David & Charles
Brunel House, Newton Abbot, Devon

CONTENTS

INTRODUCTION

Mosaic is an ancient art as can be seen from the many beautiful examples which have survived from the distant past. As well as expressing the spirit and preoccupations of the classical and Christian worlds, these mosaics also display the variety and fascination of images and patterns made up of thousands of tiny pieces. Inspired by these ancient examples, there has been a contemporary resurgence of interest in the medium of mosaic as a means of creating unique and original decorative effects while at the same time providing practical and hard-wearing surfaces.

CLASSICAL MOSAIC

The earliest known mosaics are pebble mosaics made by the Ancient Greeks in the 3rd century BC. Techniques were refined throughout the Hellenistic world and highly sophisticated and realistic panels were produced, particularly in the city of Alexandria. The idea of using mosaic as domestic decoration then spread to Italy and became widespread throughout the Roman Empire. The existence of mosaic remains is a good indicator of a period of peace and prosperity in that particular part of the Empire as the craftsmen tended to be itinerants, working wherever wealthy clients felt secure enough to invest in domestic comforts. Examples include Pompeii in the 1st century BC and North Africa in the 3rd and 4th centuries AD.

The Romans invented the idea of using mosaic on walls and vaults (see illustration 1) but these have rarely survived. The great majority of Roman mosaics take the form of pavements made from marble and other natural stones, and sometimes incorporating glass to give accents of brighter colour. Fashions varied according to time and place with geometric designs being popular in Italy, which were then superseded by black and white pictorial compositions in the 1st and

2nd centuries AD. Figurative designs executed in full colour against a plain white or cream background were popular in North Africa and spread in the 4th century AD to Sicily (see illustration 2). At the margins of the Empire, where it was harder for the skilled craftsmen to travel, geometric designs were common because they were relatively easy to make. However, there are examples of mosaics in which local craftsmen have attempted more ambitious effects, often with charming results (see illustration 3).

CHRISTIAN MOSAICS

In the early Christian era, mosaics were widely used to decorate the walls and vaults of churches and many have remained intact to this day because religious buildings have been continuously cared for and maintained. Very early examples, such as the 4th century mosaics at Santa Costanza in Rome, relate closely to secular Roman designs, but a distinctive style that expressed the didactic intention of the growing Christian church rapidly emerged and is exemplified by the great 6th century mosaics of Ravenna (see page 98). These works were designed to

1. ROMAN MOSAIC FOUNTAIN NICHE (1ST CENTURY AD)
2. OXEN TRANSPORTING WATER, PIAZZA ARMERINA, SICILY (EARLY 4TH CENTURY)
3. WOLF MOSAIC, ALDBROUGH ROMAN TOWN, YORKSHIRE (300 AD)

3

communicate the meaning of the new faith to the illiterate people through the power of their stylized and concentrated compositions; their rejection of classical realism is entirely intentional.

In medieval times, this style was developed to illustrate narrative themes from the Bible, combining naturalistic observation with simplified composition (see illustration 4, below). The Renaissance brought new techniques of painting, both in fresco and oils, and these largely superseded the expensive and difficult medium of mosaic.

MODERN MOSAICS

The great commercial wealth of late 19th century Europe allowed a revival of interest in mosaic as a decorative art to adorn its new temples of theatres and department stores. Artists and architects returned to the medium to explore its potential in the modern world. Examples of modern mosaic include the work of Antonio Gaudi in Spain and the futurists, particularly Gino Severini, in Italy. The modernist philosophy of truth to materials allowed a new and freer approach to the creation of decoration using combinations of glass, stone and ceramic. In England, the Russian emigré Boris Anrep used traditional marble cubes in figurative but astonishingly free interpretations of scenes from modern life in his great cycle of floor mosaics in the National Gallery in London (see illustration 5, right).

4

ABOUT THIS BOOK

The history of mosaic art demonstrates the great versatility of the medium but as with all disciplines it has its own strengths and weaknesses. The aim of this book is to explain and demonstrate how to use mosaic to its best advantage. Almost anything can be interpreted in mosaic but the success of the interpretation depends on an understanding of how to manipulate and control the medium. The book is divided into two sections: Principles of Design and Techniques, Tools & Materials.

Principles of Design

The first part of the book is divided into chapters covering different aspects of design: stylization, colour, contrast, laying, surface, pattern, form and figures. By separating out these issues it is possible to see how each contributes different qualities to a design; understanding this will enable you to acquire a vocabulary that will help you to create successful mosaics.

These principles are illustrated by a series of unique designs that are accompanied by method tips to enable you to reproduce them as projects. There is also a chapter devoted to deriving successful designs from historical mosaics, including three examples interpreted in modern mosaic materials.

Techniques, Tools & Materials

The second section of the book provides a comprehensive technical reference guide. Clear photographs and detailed step-by-step instructions are given for the principal mosaic methods. Descriptions of tools, adhesives, backings and mosaic materials are given in conjunction with tables explaining which will be appropriate in different applications, both

5

indoors and out. In this way, the designs illustrated in the book can be used in a wide range of different locations depending on your own particular requirements. You will also be able to work out the most suitable techniques and materials for executing your own design ideas.

Suppliers of mosaic materials are listed, and places where you can see interesting historical mosaics are recommended. Templates of some of the designs are provided so that they can be copied and used as projects.

4. NOAH TAKING THE ANIMALS INTO THE ARK, ST MARK'S, VENICE (13TH CENTURY AD)
5. EXPLORING, BORIS ANREP, NATIONAL GALLERY, LONDON (1928)

SUCCESSFUL DESIGNS COME FROM A RIGOROUSLY SELECTIVE APPROACH TO THE SUBJECT MATTER AND ITS TREATMENT. TO MAKE A STRONG IMAGE, SOME ELEMENTS WILL NEED TO BE EMPHASIZED, SOME SIMPLIFIED AND SOME LEFT OUT ALTOGETHER. IN THE BATHROOM PANEL ILLUSTRATED THE JELLYFISH AND KELP ARE DEFINED BY THEIR SHAPE ALONE. THERE ARE NO 3-D EFFECTS AS THE BACKGROUND COLOURS ARE COMPLETELY FLAT, BUT INTEREST IS ADDED BY THE SUBTLE COLOUR CHANGES FORMING PATTERNS WITHIN THE OBJECTS THEMSELVES. THIS CHAPTER LOOKS AT DIFFERENT APPROACHES TO STYLIZATION AND HOW THEY CAN BEST BE INTERPRETED IN MOSAIC TO CREATE BOTH SIMPLE AND COMPLEX EFFECTS.

1 STYLIZATION

DESIGN

The vocabulary of design is made up of four basic components and these are shape, line, form and colour. Shape describes the simple silhouette of an object. Line is used to describe its edges and those of any features it contains. The form of an object is its three-dimensional shape and it is described in two-dimensional work by use of tone or shading. Finally, there is colour and the related categories of pattern and texture that describe qualities of the object's surface.

The particular way in which you communicate the object in your design will be a matter of aesthetic choice, depending on what you are inspired by. If colour has attracted you to a particular subject, concentrate on your choice of colours to emphasize their importance; or, if the three-dimensional form was your initial inspiration, concentrate on creating the illusion of modelling with light and shade.

When creating non-representational images, considerations of recognition do not apply, leaving you freer to concentrate on the abstract attributes. Inspiration of shapes, forms and colours will be derived from the real world as

1. SHAPE

2. LINE

3. FORM

4. COLOUR

all visual imagery comes from somewhere or is suggested by something. The emphasis, however, will not be on the source of the idea but on its formal aesthetic qualities.

Your design decisions will also be influenced by the medium in which you are working. With mosaic, it is important to remember that it is an inherently busy medium because of the tracery of grout lines that will overlay any other visual effects. For this reason, and particularly when beginning to work in mosaic, it is a good idea to keep your designs simple to avoid confusion and the interference of one effect against another.

The simplest and easiest effect when working in mosaic is to change colour. In the bathroom panels pictured, the background is all laid in the same straight grid but interest is added by simply changing colour to suggest rectangular fields framing the jellyfish and the kelp. Careful selection of tonal relationships of the colours also creates the illusion that the rectangular fields are transparent because the tonal banding of the white outer background is repeated in the yellow and green banding of the boxes.

Another effect that is particularly appropriate in mosaic is pattern. Because the surface is composed of many separate elements, a simple colour change at regular intervals can be used to set up a repeating pattern. Checks, spots and crosses can be used to differentiate areas or to enliven otherwise flat expanses of colour.

Effects of light and shade can be successfully achieved in some mosaic materials but they depend on having a wide tonal range in a single colour. In vitreous glass this is possible in blues, greens and greys but more difficult in yellows, reds and oranges. In the commonly available smalti colours there are good ranges of blues, greys, reds and flesh tones but more limited greens and yellows. In marble there can be enough variation within the natural material to create a tonal sequence, for instance with carrara (white to grey) and bardiglio (pale grey to dark grey). Generally, ceramic tiles – both glazed and unglazed – do not have a wide enough colour range to allow very sophisticated tonal effects.

Linear effects can also be achieved in mosaic. Laying single, descriptive lines is almost like drawing with mosaic and is an attractively easy process. You should, however, bear in mind the problems of laying in the background. It can be quite difficult to make it look as if the lines of laying are following through a series of linear interruptions and it can also involve a lot of difficult cutting (see fig. 1). It is easier to lay in a background of random pattern in a 'crazy-paving' effect (see fig. 2).

FIG. 1

FIG. 2

Some graphic devices present particular problems in mosaic and should, if possible, be simplified or avoided altogether. Very fine lines are difficult to achieve, as are smooth blendings from one colour or tone to another. Attempting to lay a background to a very tight curve will always look awkward and lines of laying radiating out from a single point will generate a lot of difficult tapering cuts.

When making design decisions about how to stylize an image, do not be afraid to base them on what will be easy to execute in mosaic. The finished image will look natural in its technique, with an internal logic giving it an overall sense of conviction. Equally, do not feel too constrained by the appearance of the real world; use colours that work well with each other even if they do not represent the object's true appearance. Distort perspective so that it gives you interesting backgrounds in flat planes without worrying about vanishing points and tapering lines of vision. Invent generalized versions of your chosen objects, such as fish, fruit or leaves, that will give attractive shapes or lines rather than necessarily illustrating particular species or botanical types. You can repeat objects, cut them in half, or manipulate them in any way to make the image more interesting – you should feel free to make of your design whatever you want.

FRUIT & VEGETABLES

These panels show a simple but bold treatment of a series of fruit and vegetables. This is a good source of subject matter because the shapes are simple but distinctive and easily recognizable. The objects are rendered primarily through their shapes and outlines and are given more detail by being shown cut in half. This idea is then echoed by dividing the design in half and treating the two sides differently.

The overall effect of the panels is very flat as there is no use of dark and light to create form. The selection of colours is only broadly descriptive. The apple and pear are green and the pepper and tomato are red but otherwise the colours are chosen for their relationships to each other. The disposition of the colours is dictated by the need to balance the two different sides of each piece. In the apple and pear the strong dark and light contrast on one side is balanced by the vivid lime green on the other. In the tomato and pepper the fizzing brilliance of the pink and orange against the purple background is balanced by the strong contrast of the dark red lines against the pale orange.

The simple objects are further differentiated against their background by using different shaped pieces. The shapes of the fruit and vegetables are filled with triangular pieces laid in a random inter-locking arrangement. Where outlines are introduced, they are made from roughly square pieces, and the backgrounds are laid in a pattern of rectangular shapes. One of the advantages of working from larger tiles is that there is a great variety of both shapes and sizes that you can cut and use in your designs.

METHOD TIPS

• These panels are easy to make and suitable for beginners. There is no difficult cutting involved and the pieces are modest in size.

• The designs are 30cm (12in) square, but these dimensions could easily be enlarged or reduced. Being made of glazed ceramic wall tiles, they

be left off until the panel is screwed into position with countersunk screws. Keep a record of where the screws are, so that if you want to move the panels you can – bear in mind, however, that the material used makes them unsuitable for use on a floor or outdoors.

• The panels could be made using the direct method with a suitable cement-based adhesive (see page 112) or by sticking to mesh (see page 118).

• The shapes are very important in these designs so make sure that you draw a bold and pleasing outline to follow. The objects are not necessarily symmetrical but avoid unintentional irregularities.

would work well as inserts into a tiled wall, replacing a square panel of one, four or six plain tiles on a kitchen wall or splashback. If you want to insert the panels into an area of tiles that are thicker than those used in the piece you can. Remove the existing tiles and then glue the panel, backed with a thin plywood board, to the wall with contact adhesive. Alternatively, four pieces of tile in the corners of the panel could

• Start sticking the outline elements made up of square pieces and then fill in the rest of the objects with triangles. Try to keep the gaps between the tiles relatively consistent and the pieces of approximately equal size. The sudden introduction of small pieces or large gaps will catch the eye and look awkward. As a general rule, avoid using any very small pieces as they will detract from the overall simplicity of the piece as well as being difficult to stick down securely. Move on to the background, laying the rectangular pieces in different orientations on alternating rows, and introducing flashes of the contrasting colour evenly across the area.

• Black grout was chosen here to give the colours extra intensity and to emphasize the contrasting patterns of the grout lines. If you are setting the panels among other tiling, this may influence you to use another colour such as white. The effect will be less dramatic and the colours will look a little more washed out, but the designs will still read strongly and the white will give the final piece a fresh, crisp appearance.

CROCKERY TABLETOP

This design uses a variety of devices to simplify and stylize the image but the central idea was to use line, combined with colour and tone, to describe the vessels on the tabletop. The objects have been selected for their interesting outlines with the curling handles and spouts of the jugs contrasting with the gentler curves of the glass and bowl. Different coloured outlines are used on opposite sides of the objects as a stylized suggestion of light cast from one side. White outlines suggest the contrary reflectivity of glass that catches light even on the dark side of an object, while black lines add solidity and balance against the white.

Another technique used in this piece is the manipulation of perspective. Each object is framed by a rectangle of chequered pattern representing a table mat. Where these rectangles overlap, there is a colour change either to brighter or darker tones. This illusion works well against the overall flatness of the piece and sets up an effect of the different planes floating in front of each other. The conflicting perspectives of the objects seen largely side on, together with their backgrounds seen in plan or from above, confound our spatial expectations and give the piece greater liveliness.

Pattern also enlivens the surface with alternating colours creating an interesting chequer pattern. The colours are selected both to complement those used in the objects and to create a sense of balance in the overall composition. They glow with greater intensity because they are positioned against a dark background colour.

METHOD TIPS

• This piece is designed as a tabletop but it could equally well be used as a kitchen wall panel. It could be made either by sticking direct to a timber board (see page 112) or using the indirect method (see page 114). If you are making a tabletop, the indirect method has the advantage of producing a flatter surface.

• The size of the panel is 65cm (26in) square. It would be difficult to reduce the size of the design by very much without making it fiddly in execution but it could be enlarged by making all the objects on a larger scale, or by adding extra planes of flat colour or chequered pattern around the perimeter. Try to keep the overall piece a module of whole tiles, as a row of cut tiles at the edge would be out of character with the design.

• When drawing out the panel, position the jugs and dishes first and show off the curving outlines in strong, confident lines. The rectangles of the place mats can be roughly indicated and their exact position fixed only when laying in the background. Start by sticking down the outlines of the objects and then fill them in.

• Work the background by sticking a row of tiles across the top and down the side to establish the tile spacing and module. When laying the side row, remember that the plain background is offset so you need to alternate whole and half tiles. Following this spacing, you can then decide on the exact edges of the table mats and fill in accordingly. Where the grid is interrupted by objects you might find it easier to draw lines across with a ruler to make sure that they run straight.

• If you have used the indirect method, stand back when you have finished the piece to check that your colour selection, particularly in the chequered patterns, creates a balanced whole. Some areas may contrast too strongly, while others may be too muted. Changes can easily be made at this stage: apply a damp cloth or sponge to the back of the paper, leave this for 15 to 20 minutes to loosen the glue, then you can remove selected tiles without tearing the paper.

SUMMER

This mosaic is an interpretation of a landscape in summer and although it is very stylized it is immediately recognizable. The most important aspect of this design is the use of pattern. Each distinct area has its own pattern, generated by a combination of colour changes and varieties of laying. The field areas tend to have smaller scale patterns laid in rows in one or two directions, helping to differentiate them from the wilder patterns of the trees with their swirls and curving lines. Much of the piece is made up of close tones of blues and greens and it is the different patterns that are used to differentiate one area from another.

In the overall blue-green composition very bright colours are introduced, sometimes as elements of the patterns and sometimes as whole fields. These flashes of brightness combined with the occasional use of white give a sense of sunlight suffusing the landscape. All the colour combinations, whether between vivid blues and greens or strong lime greens and olives, produce a hot, shimmering effect where the indistinct boundaries of the colours suggest the distortions of heat haze.

Although there is no three-dimensional modelling, the picture is not flat. The composition tells us through the position of the curving hills that they lie one in front of the other, and a sense of perspective is implied, although largely hidden, by the blocks of trees. The orange field in the middle of the picture draws the eye in, as if glimpsed through steep and wooded hills.

METHOD TIPS

• This complicated piece involves sophisticated colour selections and careful cutting so is better suited to more experienced mosaicists. It is designed as a framed panel, 70cm (28in) square, but could be fixed to a wall, perhaps in a garden, to create the illusion of a distant view. It can be made using either the direct or indirect method (see pages 112 and 114).

• Before you begin, save yourself time and distraction by cutting a supply of quartered vitreous glass tiles in advance.

• When sticking down the pieces, work on one area at a time, always paying attention to the colour of adjacent areas. You need to maintain the careful balance between keeping some neighbouring colours close in tone or hue and at the same time marking the clear definition of the separate areas. Remember that the lines of laying will also help to differentiate one area from another.

• From a purely visual point of view, this piece will work well ungrouted. There may be practical considerations, such as ease of cleaning, but if the piece is to be hung as a picture you may prefer the more intense appearance of an ungrouted mosaic. If you are not grouting, the vitreous glass can be used the other way up to give the piece an overall texture. Using the direct method, the glass sticks better with its flat face down and if the tesserae are carefully cut the gaps between can be virtually invisible. This means that the colours are in direct contact with each other and, without the intervening neutral colour of the grout, they can glow more brightly.

GALLERY

THE POTATO COD & BARRACUDA

These panels (below) are part of the bathroom shown at the beginning of this chapter (see page 10). The fish are described by a combination of shape and pattern. The barracuda are repeated and carefully grouped to suggest the synchronized movements of a shoal and the individual fish have a simple pattern of stripes on their backs. The potato cod, in contrast, occupies his panel in solitary splendour, his bulky shape enlivened by his blobby and irregular markings. All these panels incorporate lettering which is a device often found in ancient mosaics. As well as allowing for the introduction of interesting words, the colour and shape of the letters and their positioning across the panels add an extra visual element to the design. Silver tiles are used in the background of the cod panel to give the piece sparkle, and these are echoed in the occasional mirror tile set into the surrounding white field.

THE LIBRARY SHOWER

This small shower room (above) leads off a library and the client hoped that the function of the room would not be too obvious. The solution was to decorate the walls as if they were an extension of the library itself with books and curios arranged on shelves. Only a small range of colours has been used and the walls have been given a very clear structure by sub-division into a series of panels. There are no fussy details or three-dimensional effects and the design works as a series of simple, flat panels that do not overpower the confined space that they decorate.

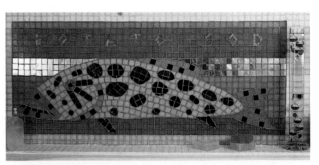

FOOD PANELS

These panels were part of a series designed to hang on the walls of a restaurant. They show the progression of buying, preparing, cooking, presenting and eating food. Although this is a relatively static subject, the client wanted the designs to convey a sense of movement. Rather than going for food fights or kitchen disasters, the panels have been animated by a dynamic design treatment, with objects positioned at conflicting angles and the patterned background cloths distorted into irregular shapes. The bowls and dishes have very simple shapes but also strong, three-dimensional forms created by the tonal transitions from dark to light.

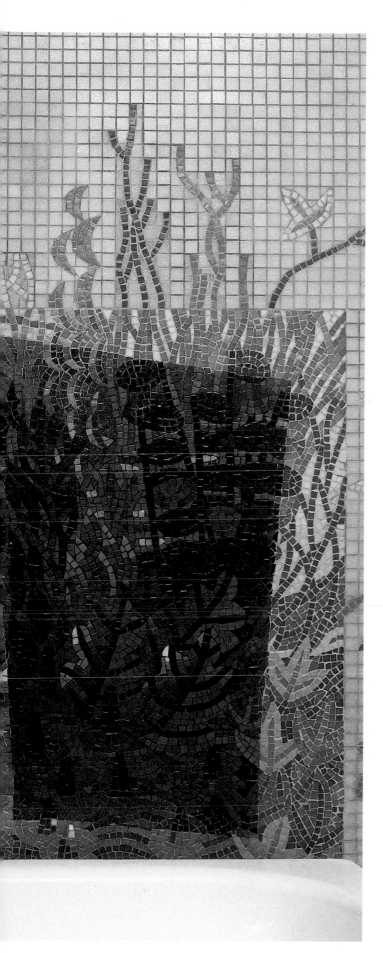

LEARNING HOW TO USE AND
APPRECIATE COLOUR IS ONE
OF THE MOST ENJOYABLE
ASPECTS OF WORKING IN
MOSAIC. THIS PANEL, MADE
FOR A BATHROOM WALL,
DEMONSTRATES BRIGHT
AND MUTED COLOURS, AS
WELL AS MONOTONE IN ONE
PIECE. IT ALSO USES SEVERAL
TONES OF GROUT, WHICH HAS
A FAR GREATER IMPACT ON
THE WAY IN WHICH WE SEE
COLOURS THAN YOU MIGHT
THINK. THIS CHAPTER EXPLAINS
SOME COMMON COLOUR
TERMINOLOGY, DISCUSSES THE
IMPORTANCE OF MAKING
PREPARATORY COLOURED
DRAWINGS, AND EXPLAINS THE
COLOUR CHARACTERISTICS OF
VARIOUS MOSAIC MATERIALS,
INCLUDING THE ADVANTAGES,
DISADVANTAGES AND SUITABLE
APPLICATIONS OF EACH.

2 COLOUR

EXPLORING COLOUR

When talking about colour, the terms 'hue', 'tone' and 'intensity' are often referred to. A definition of each can be very helpful when learning about mosaic design.

HUE

The hue of a colour is the place it has in the colour spectrum, for example blue, yellow or red. There is a variety of traditions about colour which try to define successful combinations. The idea of complementary colours is just one of these. Complementaries are those colours which oppose one another in the colour wheel, for example red and green. In this book, we also use the term to refer to colours like brown and purple, which are mixed colours and cannot be found in the spectrum, and achromatic colours (colours without hue) such as black, white and grey.

TONE

Tone is an important issue to consider if you want to make your mosaic comprehensible. In this book, all discussion of tone is divided into three sections: light tones, mid tones and dark or bright tones. Imagine that you wish to make a mosaic with adjacent objects defined by different colours. They may be individually distinct in terms of hue, but if they are tonally close they will be drawn together, which might lose the definition between them. There are measures you can take to remedy the situation if you spot this happening. It is possible to increase definition by laying tiles of the same hue but gradating them through lighter or darker tones where the areas adjoin. Another way to mark the distinction between one colour and another is by altering the laying method. You could change the direction of the tiles, for example, or perhaps outline them. These methods aimed at increasing clarity come from experience, and with practice you will be able to invent others of your own.

INTENSITY

The intensity of a colour is its degree of colour saturation, or colour weight. The colour intensity of an area affects how a mosaic balances, as more intense colours seem weightier than less saturated ones. This does not, however, mean that intensity refers only to dark colours – brilliant white is really striking and intense, as is lemon yellow.

If you squint your eyes and look at a mosaic colour chart, the intense colours are the ones that jump out at you. These are generally the brights, which tend to be the most expensive mosaic tiles. Oddly enough, there are colours such as the bright blues and greens which can be made to look contextually intense, but do not have permanent colour weight or they can be combined with other tiles to make them look muted and you can demonstrate this for yourself by making experimental mixes. Fix a small sample panel of strong blues and greens – you will notice that over a distance they tend to merge, even to lose their colour and become rather grey. The place in the spectrum where you might expect them to interrelate somehow changes. This is often partly to do with the grout colour and does not happen to intense colours, which retain their purity. Do remember, however, that intensity is comparative. A colour that might seem pale and mild in one context can seem powerful when used with others of a lower tonal value than itself.

THIS COLLECTION OF TILES IS PALE IN TONE. THERE IS COLOUR
VARIATION, BUT TONAL SIMILARITY. THE GREY AND GREEN ALMOST
MERGE TONALLY, BUT THE WHITE IS LIGHTER. THIS MAKES IT STAND
OUT AND INTRODUCES A FRESHNESS TO THE MIX.

THIS COMBINATION OF DARK AND MID TONES PRODUCES AN
ATTRACTIVE FLICKERY EFFECT. TAKE CARE TO ENSURE A MIX LIKE THIS
BALANCES ACROSS THE WHOLE AREA AS A SUDDEN PATCH OF
DARKER OR LIGHTER TILES CAN LOOK RATHER STRANGE.

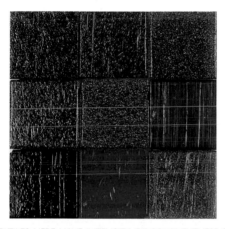

THE RED TILES HERE HAVE INTENSITY OF COLOUR. THESE SEEM
VIBRANT AGAINST A DARK AND RATHER MUTED BACKGROUND
MIXTURE. WITHOUT THE RED, THE PURPLY BLUE COLOUR WOULD
READ AS MUCH MORE INTENSE.

THE BLUE AND OLIVE GREEN HERE ARE VERY CLOSE IN TONE.
COLOURS WHICH ARE TONALLY CLOSE HAVE A TENDENCY TO FUSE
TOGETHER AT A DISTANCE.

THIS PANEL IS DARK IN TONE. UNLESS TILES HAVE A STRONG
INTENSITY OF COLOUR, THE TENDENCY OF CLOSE TONES TO FUSE
CAN LEAD TO A COLOUR MIX SEEMING RATHER GREY. THE GREY
USED IN THIS MIXTURE WILL INCREASE THE LIKELIHOOD OF THIS.

THIS PANEL EFFECTIVELY DEMONSTRATES THE FACT THAT INTENSITY
IS A DIFFERENT THING FROM BRIGHTNESS. THE CENTRAL
BROWN/GREEN TILE HAS ALMOST AS MUCH INTENSITY AS THE
BRIGHT COLOURS.

GROUT

It is remarkable how much one's perception of colour in a mosaic is altered by grout. When people think of mosaic, they often imagine impressionist or pointillist colour – lots of tiny adjacent dots of brightness. In fact, it is rare for any mosaic tile to be adjacent to another without the intervening medium of grout – so, instead of the effect being like a painting by Seurat, it is more like a Seurat painting covered in a grey, black or white mesh. It is not hard to see that this profoundly alters colour relationships, and that grout mutes the luminosity and vibrancy of the tiles.

Compare the sample panels opposite. All four panels contain colours of identical colours, but we read them quite differently because of the grout colour. These samples do have scope for misinterpretation. Do not conclude from looking at this, for example, that white grout is always very fracturing, or that dark grout always provides high contrast. If you look further at these sample panels, you will see that all four grouts can be used with subtlety.

There is a general rule that you should grout a mosaic using the principal tone used in the piece. So, if predominantly pale tones have been used, choose a white or ivory grout; if mainly mid tones were used, grout it grey; and if the mosaic is principally dark, grout it black. These four grouts are adequate for the needs of most mosaics. If a piece has high tonal contrast, for example black and white, it would be grouted in mid grey, so that both colours were broken up equally. Obviously, there are exceptions to these rules – you may wish, for example, to foreground one image and fracture another – but it is a useful rule of thumb.

UNGROUTED MOSAIC

If you want vibrant, luminous colour, unmuted by a matrix of a single tone, make your piece and do not grout it. This does have practical consequences: it is not really suitable for floors and is also tricky, although not impossible, to use outside because in winter, water may freeze instead of running out of the joints, causing pieces to come adrift. Assess how practical an ungrouted mosaic would be for the location you wish to use it.

PLANNING COLOURS

Drawing up a design and planning colours helps to iron out any problems you may encounter, and it is often easier and quicker to solve a problem on paper than with a large mosaic. Here are some tips to help you make a successful working drawing:

• Select a palette of coloured tiles, then find a medium such as paint with a range which matches that of your mosaic tiles. Choose one which reproduces as closely as possible the discrete flat colour effects of mosaic. Remember that your palette is fixed, and you cannot mix and meld colour as you can with other mediums. Even subtle colour transitions are quite difficult to make unless the work is very large and likely to be seen from a distance.

• Do not be tempted to compromise the selection of tiles you have made for the sake of an attractive drawing. If, in reality, you plan to use a vivid red, make sure it looks as vivid on your drawing as it does in reality. If you do not use the correct colours, you will not be able to spot any potential problems of balance, and will therefore be cheated out of finding a solution.

These panels are a random mix of colours divided into four panels and grouted in four tones of grout. The tile colours are identical, although they are not in the same position on the board. The visual effect is altered by the grout colour. The light tones emphasize different properties of colour from the dark ones. Although the general rule is to grout a mosaic in its principal tone, it may be hard to make a decision when there are sharply contrasting tones within one piece. In this case, it is generally most effective if the mosaic is grouted a tone mid-way between the two.

WHITE GROUT: ALTHOUGH THIS HAS A VERY FRACTURING EFFECT, IT DOES EMPHASIZE THE HUE OF THE TILES.

IVORY GROUT: THIS IS SLIGHTLY SOFTER IN EFFECT THAN WHITE GROUT.

GREY GROUT: GREY GROUT WORKS VERY WELL WITH MID TONE TILES. DIFFERENT GREY GROUTS ALSO HAVE DIFFERENT QUALITIES, SOME BEING BROWNER THAN OTHERS.

DARK GROUT: THIS EFFECT IS GENERALLY CLOSEST TO UNGROUTED MOSAIC. ALTHOUGH IT MAY LOOK MURKY AT FIRST, DARK GROUT LIGHTENS AS IT DRIES.

BIRD TILE

This tile of a pelican demonstrates some simple principles involving colour. The bird is laid against a background which is relatively close in tone to the colour of its body. If you use colours which are tonally very close, you can have problems with making an image clearly readable. But although there is a potential loss through an image being unclear, there is something attractive about the subtlety of using close tones. This pelican is very simple and stylized, and is treated with flat areas of colour. It gains something from the contrast between the closely related tones of background and bird, and the bright colour of its legs and beak. The bird's body is laid in a contrasting way to that of the background, and this helps to keep the image comprehensible.

The pelican is made in vitreous glass – probably the best choice if you are interested in experimenting with colour. It is relatively inexpensive, has a broad colour palette and can be used to create a wide range of effects.

METHOD TIPS

This decorative tile could be used on a wall, or it could equally well serve as a practical object, like a pot stand. Where an item has a practical function like this, it is not advisable to have tiny cuts abutting an edge, as these are vulnerable to being knocked off. This design has a border of whole tiles which protects any tiles you plan to cut. This piece is ideal for a beginner and can be made using the direct or indirect method (see pages 112 and 114).

• Choose your range of colours carefully. This mosaic is held together by the choice of grout colour which is close in tone to the colours used in the tile. You may well wish to choose an entirely different range of colours. If you do so, remember that if you select tesserae which have strong tonal contrast, the grout you use may unite one area while dividing another, therefore upsetting the balance of your design. See Grout (page 26) for further advice.

• When selecting colours, bear in mind the tonal characteristics of the tiles you are planning to use. It is not only by choosing close tones that you can encounter problems with clarity, but also with dramatically contrasting ones. Where a wide range of different tones is used, the image can seem difficult to read, becoming rather spotty and unclear. Select across a wide tonal range only when you want contrast or colour variation.

GLAZED CERAMIC TABLETOP

Glazed ceramic tiles are available in a wide variety of different colours, patterns and finishes. They can be extremely enjoyable to work with as the range they offer is so broad, and the scope for possible mosaic treatments so varied. Working from larger units, you can create the sizes of tile and kinds of cut that you want. There are only a couple of significant limits to their range of applications. One comes from the fact that they are generally only glazed on one side, so using them in reverse is very difficult. The other main limit is the fact that many of the broadest ranges of colours are interior wall tiles, which are not suitable for use outside or on floors. Often the glaze is rather weakened in its adhesion to the tile body once it has been cut, so it is a good idea to check that the material is appropriate for the task you wish it to perform.

This glazed ceramic tabletop shows quite a free approach to cutting and colour. The pattern is based on dividing the circle into sections. A repeating shape radiates from the centre, and enters a central band where it changes tone. The tabletop is based on experimenting with increasing and diminishing the intensity of colours used. It is very simple, but produces a surprisingly interesting effect. Remember that simple ideas can be effective, and that complexity does not necessarily improve a good idea.

METHOD TIPS

This project, made using the direct method (see page 112), requires a degree of skill in cutting and laying to achieve the effects shown.

• It can sometimes prove difficult to make a successful colour selection of tiles. Working with a piece which depends more on the interrelationship between colours than it does on design or execution, it is important to be sure that your choice is as exciting as possible. Hold your colours up to one another: compare the frisson that one set of choices gives you in comparison to another. You will notice how lively some combinations seem while others simply appear flat. To people born with a good sense of colour it probably seems obvious, but for some of us, colour sense is only acquired by looking and learning in this way. Once you have begun to notice how colour works, you will find it endlessly interesting.

• Take care when choosing your grout colour. This mosaic is unified by the grout, although a dramatically contrasting grout could be effective, as it would emphasize the fractured nature of the design. Using the darkest grout, as here, helps to emphasize the intense band of colour at the centre of the table. If this piece had been grouted grey, the background colours would have looked softer and more unified, but it would have slightly diminished the intensity of the bright band at the centre. Grouting it in white, on the other hand, would have made the whole piece read as broken and fractured, placing the emphasis on the cutting rather than the colour.

CERAMIC MIRROR

The characteristics of unglazed ceramic are demonstrated by this mirror which shows the soft, matt, earthy tones of the material. The subtle colours are boosted by being accompanied by white tiles. Ceramic is very often used for floors where it is difficult to use high or intense colour. If you wish to make the colours seem stronger, use black and/or white with them as they always intensify the colours they accompany.

Ceramic has another feature which relates to its flat, neutral shades: its subtlety draws attention to the way it is jointed. This is not so much the case with glass mosaic, where the glossiness and lively colour distracts attention from the spacing. Thus it is less easy to disguise cutting errors with ceramic than it is with glass or marble. None of the projects in this chapter is made with marble, but it might be useful to know how it differs from ceramic. Although the two materials have certain similarities, the natural veining and mottling of marble make it look less flat than ceramic. This mottling draws attention away from the cuts, which can be an advantage. It is also worth noting that ceramic is easier to cut than marble or glass. Try to use the inherent qualities of every material so you benefit from their differences. For example, if ceramic focuses attention on the joints, use it where the joints are a significant design feature.

METHOD TIPS

This project requires a level of skill in cutting to produce the most effective results, so it is probably a good idea to try it after you have developed your confidence a little. It is made using the direct method (see page 112).

• Use the grout to unify the design. The mid tones in this mosaic are united by grey grout. The delicate silhouettes of the trees are drawn together in a fine tracery, set against the contrasting colour of the background. This is fractured by the grey grout, which at the same time unites the trees into stronger single shapes. Most of the tree trunks are grey, but the fish motif in the bottom central panel shows that the mid green and blue can be pulled together by grey grout in the same way.

• Design the shapes and forms specifically with this piece in mind. The mosaic is planned to an exact tile module (a whole cut tile repeat) and the design is divided into sections which express the geometry of both mirror and border.

GALLERY

MARBLE & SMALTI GARDEN MOSAIC

This piece shows how effective an ungrouted mosaic can be. It was made with the aim of introducing texture, colour and structure into a small garden. The mosaic was placed opposite a beautiful flint wall, and from the house you could see a large, old, rusty-coloured pantiled roof. The piece echoes this colour and texture, and the design is structured to give a sense of an espaliered tree, growing against a wall. The colour in the garden was generally muted, and the client wanted some strong, vibrant colour to brighten up the garden, particularly in winter. The design is subdivided into areas of extreme intensity, and the leaves are given an abstract overlay in a series of geometric shapes. The intensely coloured smalti has been muted by combining it with the earthy, softer tones of marble. The contrast between the smalti's intense, reflective surface, and the matt, light-absorbent, riven face of the marble has an effect which is complementary to both materials.

BATHROOM PANEL

This mosaic is made with vitreous glass and the shapes are based on natural forms. The room in which the mosaic was placed was at the top of the house, and had a sloping roof. The angled shapes are picked up by the mosaic, and a mirror was specially cut to fit in with the curves and angles of the forms. Here you can see how intense orange and brilliant white provide lively colour set against the softer, mid-toned background.

FISH MEN

This mosaic demonstrates the intensity and liveliness of smalti – a material made of enamelled glass and often seen in Byzantine mosaics. Other than silver and gold leaf, it is probably the most expensive of mosaic materials. Its possible applications are limited by a fractured textured surface, pitted with little holes. It can only really be used on walls where slightly rough and potentially sharp finish will not be a problem. Smalti is generally left ungrouted, as the tiny holes fill up with grout which mutes the colour. Its most defining characteristic is a powerful intensity of colour which makes it difficult to use. It retains great strength of colour over distance, so its traditional use on domes and high ceilings makes sense. Here, the fractured face is light-reflective and the highly saturated blue is softened by the use of grey.

CONTRAST IN MOSAIC HAS MANY ASPECTS. IT CAN APPLY TO TONE, MATERIAL, TREATMENT, SURFACE AND COLOUR. HERE, A MOSAIC OF A GARDEN PAVEMENT DEMONSTRATES JUST HOW EFFECTIVE TONAL CONTRAST CAN BE WHERE STRAIGHT-LAID, BLACK MARBLE AND BANDS OF WHITE MARBLE CUBES ARE SET AGAINST AREAS OF GREEN GLASS CUBES. THIS CHAPTER LEADS YOU THROUGH VARIOUS DIFFERENT CUTTING METHODS USED TO CREATE SECTIONS OF CONTRASTING SIZE, SHAPE AND EDGING WHICH CAN THEN BE INCORPORATED IN MOSAICS TO SUPPORT AND ENHANCE OTHER CONTRASTING ASPECTS WITHIN THE WHOLE, FINISHED PIECE.

3 CONTRAST

CREATING CONTRAST BY CUTTING

There is a range of contrasting shapes you can use in your mosaic. Most people can probably think of three ways of using mosaic. The first is to use the material as it comes from the factory. The second is to quarter-cut it. The third is to cut it in a haphazard way, as if it had been broken accidentally (this is sometimes described as being Gaudiesque). In fact, there is an almost infinite number of ways in which you can cut mosaic pieces.

Over the past few decades, mosaic has been subject to certain fashions in decoration. In the 1950s, for example, contrast was considered important and mosaics produced during this period tend to show wide differences in scale: small tiles used with large ones, half tiles contrasting with quarter-cut ones, and unreflective materials cut to highlight the glossiness of others. Also popular was textural contrast. You often see materials used for their linearity, such as lead, contrasting with materials used for flatness, such as slate. This way of working probably comes from an idea which was a common currency of modernism, namely truth to materials. A craftsperson would aim to distil the essential character of any material. A piece of slate or chalk used in a mosaic should reveal itself as slaty or chalky to the maximum extent.

By the 1960s, the fashion in mosaic was to show how it had entered the modern world: its appeal was that it looked manmade. Mosaic was used to clad subways, tower blocks and vast exterior walls. Cutting was

DIRECTIONAL LAYING CONTRAST

not really an issue, as the fashion was for rigidly geometrical glass, supplied on sheets straight from the factory. The 1970s and early 1980s were a fallow period, and suppliers and manufacturers survived by appealing to the swimming-pool market. Enthusiasm for modernism began to wane as buildings and

TILE SIZE CONTRAST

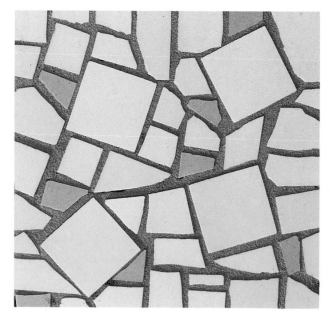

CUTTING CONTRAST — LARGE AND SMALL CUTS

subways clad in mosaic began to look less sleek, and more scruffy.

But by the mid-1980s there was a resurgence of interest in handmade items. Craft production seemed an attractive alternative to the impersonal face of industry. Two trends began, with roughly equal

MATERIAL CONTRAST — GLASS AND CERAMIC

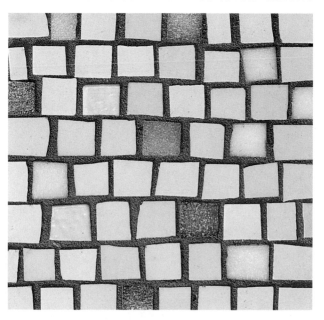

fashion currency. One was for mosaic made from marble and natural materials, which referred nostalgically to an ancient heritage. The other was for the busy, fractured, contemporary look of broken tile mosaic, whose mentor was Gaudi. In both cases the aim was to produce something which looked as if no machine could have done it, and contrasting materials, patterns and sizes of pieces were part of its attraction. Haphazardly laid mosaic can work well if it is randomly laid within a rigid system and this was just how Gaudi's ceramicist, Josep Maria Jujol, used it. The famous serpentine benches of the Park Guell are predominantly white, their flowing forms studded throughout with ovid forms, again all laid in white ceramic. The colour where it occurs and the fracturing of the tiles is undeniably free, but it is subject to rules. It is not, as it is sometimes interpreted, just a matter of throwing everything into the mix. This is probably the most important rule in using contrast successfully. You need a system within which oppositions can then work successfully. Making visually appealing contrast is not a matter of anything goes.

By the arrival of the 1990s, mosaic itself was fashionable — it stood for something, while at the same time its role as a cultural metaphor broadened the ways it could be used. Suddenly almost any approach was allowed. Now must be an ideal time to work in mosaic. If you study the following examples, you will notice how varied the effects of differing cuts can be. Think of the joints between the tiles as something like the marks made by a pen on a piece of paper. The comparison might help you to see the great breadth of possibilities open to you.

GLAZED
TILE TABLETOP

This piece demonstrates various kinds of contrast. One is that of the size of pieces. The light, central area is cut in a free, fairly unstructured way, using the tiles just as they happen to break, and not aiming to create any particular kind of effect. The border is more formally arranged. Once again, there is a band of contrasting colour which has a tonal or colour relationship with its immediate surroundings, although what the relationship is varies around the tabletop. The pieces are cut to create a series of patterns, some with extreme colour contrast. The oranges and yellows are bright and so stand out, whereas the maroon and black have a powerful density of colour. The border does balance overall, in spite of the fact that this is achieved by various means. It is useful to notice that balance does not have to be achieved by symmetry, or even by echoing colours and shapes. It can come instead from colour weight and shape.

METHOD TIPS

This project is made with glazed ceramic tiles which can break in unpredictable ways. Some experience is required in cutting this material.

• As this piece is made from glazed ceramic tiles it can only really be made using the direct method (see page 112). It is possible to stick the tile on to mesh, but they would not be suitable for use outside because the glue is not weather-proof. It is difficult to use glazed ceramic tiles in reverse, as obviously you are unable to see what the colours are.

• Glazed tiles break in an unpredictable way to produce irregular shapes. The border is grouted black, which unites the bright and deeper colours. The centre is also grouted black, which emphasizes the joints and the slightly haphazard cutting. The centre of this table was, in fact, made twice. The first time the tiles were scored and broken, and the effect was very mechanical looking. The centre of the table looked too contrived for the rather free cutting around the border, so it was remade with a looser approach which sits with the border much more effectively.

• Glazed ceramic tiles are soft and easy to cut, so you can really vary the shapes and sizes of tesserae. When the material you are using is small, like most mosaic tiles, there is not much scope for experiment and all areas have to be finely cut. Larger ceramic tiles, though, offer far more freedom and whole areas of background can be cut from a single piece. This gives a different kind of effect from most mosaic making.

FISH MOSAIC

This panel demonstrates a simple binary opposition of black and white. The fish are reversed and the colours opposed. A schematic design like this depends on one or two simple contrasts to work effectively. One is obviously the strong tonal contrast, but another is the way in which the tiles are laid. The bodies of the fish curve in opposition to the wave-like curve of the background. Cutting the tiles to points along the spiny backs of the fishes contrasts with the regular, quarter-tile size of the unglazed ceramic, and sets up a spiky rhythm which the curving wave then follows. The contrasting size of the tile module (a quarter-tile which has been quartered again) helps to make the upper fish appear particularly lively. Many ancient mosaics were made in black and white. A limited palette allows you to concentrate on the way the tiles are cut and to create internal patterns for individual areas. It would be possible, for example, to cut all the tiles on the bodies of the fish into slivers, reminiscent of fish skeletons.

METHOD TIPS

This panel is about 30cm (12in) square and can be made using either direct or indirect method (see pages 112 and 114). The piece is fairly simple to do, but you will need to master some intricate cutting to make it work effectively.

• Start by laying and sticking the outer lines of the fish, which are critical to the success of the design. Once the outer skeletal lines are laid you can fill in the bodies. Start from the base of the upper fish, so you do not have to make two rows of small cuts where the same colour meets. If any fine cutting is necessary, do it in the middle where it is easiest to disguise.

• Once the fish are complete, start laying the tiles at the junction of the black and white. This means that neither colour is cut at the point where they meet, which might give an impression of one tone being of greater significance than another. Working back from a central line like this does inevitably mean producing cut tiles along an edge. These are vulnerable, and may well fall off if the mosaic gets knocked, so if you plan to use your mosaic for a practical purpose like a pot stand, it would probably be sensible to make the whole thing slightly smaller, and surround it with a protective border.

• If the mosaic was grouted to match one of the two tile colours, one part of the mosaic would be prioritized, which could potentially put the mosaic out of balance. A much safer option is to grout it grey. This breaks up both the black and white equally. Even when using close-toned colours, this rule can still apply. Mix a colour mid-way between the two, remembering to keep a record of the proportions that you use.

MARBLE GARDEN TABLE

This mosaic was made as a table for the garden of a beautiful Queen Anne house. The garden walls and terrace on which the table stood were shades of grey and white, and the walls of the house were soft red in colour. The muted shades of the marble and the fairly traditional treatment fitted the formality of the house and garden. The mosaic demonstrates how rich a simple contrast of tone can be, and how it can give a sense of depth and complexity.

It is worth pointing out that this piece was remade. Initially the arms of the sun were laid along the lines by which they radiate out, while the background was laid as it is here, in a series of circles. This was a laying contrast which did not work. Having to cut along all the junctions between tones made the mosaic look uneven and scrappy and the tonal bands looked random and rather haphazard. Fortunately, we had not made up very much of the design before it became obvious that it was not going to work. The design was remade so it was all expressed in a series of circles, which looked much clearer. The moral of this story is to be alert to the fact that contrast for its own sake is not necessarily a virtue.

METHOD TIPS

This table is made from honed marble, with its naturally muted colours. When it rains, however, the mosaic colours become more intense, and the character of the whole piece changes. Cutting marble is more difficult than cutting vitreous glass, and a high level of skill is needed before attempting this project which should be made using the indirect method (see page 114).

• If you want to make a mosaic garden table, think carefully about the support and base. The most suitable material from which to make the support is sand and cement, reinforced with stainless steel. This stands up well to the elements, but it is heavy and needs to be supported by a strong table base. Wood is a sensible choice but you must use marine ply, with a hardwood frame for the tabletop, as softwood would certainly rot outside.

• This table plays with contrasts of various kinds. One is the opposition between plain areas of dark and light marble – a simple graphic device which always works well in black and white.

• Another kind of contrast is between mid tones and darker and lighter areas. This gives a sense of depth, and the rather milky astral associations the grey marble has are appropriate for the sun and moon theme of the mosaic.

• Closer to the edge of the table the plain areas of black marble are broken by spots of white. This simple contrast of size and pattern is intended to remind you of specks of starlight in a night sky.

GALLERY

ENTRANCE TO THE GROUCHO CLUB

There is obviously a contrast between black and white here, but there is also a contrast of how the tiles are cut. The mosaic is made up from a series of patterns formed by cut tiles. The black and white patterns of the crocodile overlap the black and white patterns of the background. This is potentially confusing to look at and it is only the pattern contrast which makes it possible to identify the creature. Although it might have been easier to see what the animal was if it had been outlined, the complexity of the image is, in itself, part of the mosaic's appeal.

DIAMONDS

This simple mosaic uses contrasting shapes and tones. A series of diamond shapes are divided into triangles and used first on one axis and then on another. Like the marble garden table, the panel shows how grey marble can give a sense of transparency when used together with black and white. By moving the same colours around the piece and arranging them in various combinations, you can observe the intensifying effect of black and white on colour. Look how differently the yellow marble reads next to the grey as opposed to the black. Experiment with simple colour and tonal exercises like these for yourself. You will be surprised by how much you can learn.

MOTH TABLE AND SWIRL TABLE

This marble garden table uses the mottled effect of the material and the skeining nature of the cuts to describe the camouflaged and veined impression of moths' wings. The table is grouted grey which is similar in tone to the brown of the moths. It fractures the black background and makes the moths look as if they have been caught in a net. The significant contrasts used here are between the figured marble used for the insects and the flat black of the background. The contrast between the smaller cuts of the wings and the larger cubes used for the background help to emphasize their fragility.

This simple, swirl marble table is based on the pattern created by a single circling line. The grey grout fractures the black and white evenly.

THE WAY IN WHICH MOSAIC IS
LAID AND THE LINES THAT IT
FOLLOWS IS CALLED *ANDAMENTI*.
THESE LINES ARE A UNIQUE
CHARACTERISTIC OF MOSAIC
AND FORM AN IMPORTANT
ELEMENT IN BOTH THE DESIGN
AND EXECUTION OF A PIECE.
GROUT LINES SET UP PATTERN
AND RHYTHM; STRAIGHT ONES
CREATE A STRUCTURED FORMAL
EFFECT, WHILE CURVED LINES
SUGGEST MOVEMENT AND
ANIMATION. THIS CHAPTER
EXPLORES A WHOLE RANGE
OF LAYING METHODS, WHICH
CAN BE USED INDIVIDUALLY
OR COMBINED TOGETHER TO
CREATE DIFFERENT EFFECTS.
IN THE ENTRANCE FLOOR
PICTURED, THE BACKGROUND
IS LAID IN A TRADITIONAL FAN
DESIGN WHERE THE GROUT
LINES ALONE CREATE A
DISTINCTIVE PATTERN.

4 LAYING

LAYING TIPS

1

4

This chapter concentrates on the methods of laying tiles that are either square in shape or cut from square tiles. Many other shapes can be used (see Chapter 3), but manufactured mosaics are usually square and this is the traditional shape of most tesserae. Some mosaic techniques work against the visibility of grout lines and should be avoided if you are making a virtue of the laying technique. Grout that is close in tone to the tile colour will disguise the joints, while the use of a mixture of colours will create a flickering effect that will be stronger than the grout lines in between. An example of this is the random mixes of colours often found in swimming pools, where the colour variation creates a stronger pattern than the simple grid on which the tiles are laid.

There are various factors involved in deciding which line to follow in laying your design but a good way to start is to think of the line which will involve the least cutting. This is not as lazy as it sounds since the simplest solution often looks the most natural and elegant. There may, however, be other considerations. The direction of laying can be used to differentiate one area from another or to establish a relationship between areas of different colour. In some designs it may be appropriate to select a line that represents the direction of movement, for instance birds flying through the air or fish swimming through water.

Different lines of movement can be combined in a single design as can be seen in the entrance floor pictured at the beginning of this chapter, where the sea creatures are arranged according to their own movement across the fan-laid background, which represents the movement of the waves.

2

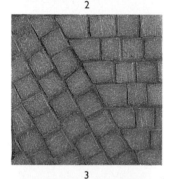

3

5

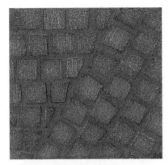

6

7

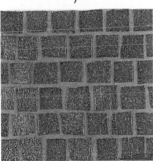

8

9

10

SMALL PIECES

It is best to avoid using tiny pieces of tile in a design (fig 1) for two reasons. First, they are difficult to fix and, second, they can look ugly because of the proportionately large amount of grout around them.

There are two techniques you can use to avoid small pieces. You can either insert a half-tile before the cut (fig 2), or, if you are working from larger tiles, you can cut a special long piece (fig 3).

JUNCTIONS

In whole tile work, try to avoid creating a line where two cut faces meet as the joint can be irregular and ugly (fig 4). This can be avoided by changing the direction of the *andamenti* in the adjacent area so that the tiles remain whole on one side (fig 5).

ANGLES

When you are fitting pieces of tile next to an angled line, take care not to cut the tiles unevenly, thus creating steps in the line (fig 6). The eye will read the line made by the edge of the tiles. It is therefore important to make a line that is continuous (fig 7).

JOINT WIDTH

Joints between tiles can be of almost any width as long as they are consistent within a piece (figs 8 and 9). However, laying tiles so that a variety of widths is created within a single piece will look unintentional and messy (fig 10).

In small pieces up to 45cm (18in) square it is possible to lay the tiles without any joints at all. In larger pieces, grout joints are necessary to take up any differential movement between the backing and the tiles. In very large panels, movement joints should be provided at 3m (10ft) intervals. Movement joints are wide, vertical joints filled with a mastic sealant.

BACKGROUNDS

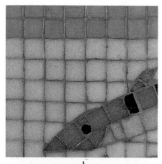

1

2

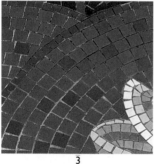

3

4

5

6

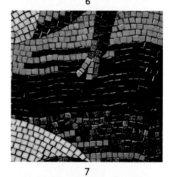

7

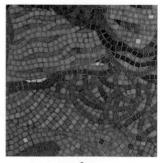

8

STRAIGHT-LAID IN BOTH DIRECTIONS

This is useful if you are setting a design into sheeted-up mosaic but can leave very small pieces and difficult cuts around the outline of inserted shapes (fig. 1).

OFFSET

With this method joints do not have to be vertically aligned, you can start a row with a convenient cut and follow curving and diagonal lines (fig. 2).

FAN

This pattern is set up using a compass. Draw in extra guidelines to avoid starting at the top and ending up nowhere near the 'keystone' piece at the bottom (fig. 3).

OPUS VERMICULATUM

In this type of background, worm-like lines of mosaic follow the outline of the object, emphasizing its shape and separating it from the background (fig. 4).

OUTLINING

Outlining shapes in the background colour first will give a tidy joint around the edge of any object and help disguise the cut line against tiles of the same colour. It is a technique often used in lettering (fig. 5).

CIRCLES

When making a circular mosaic, draw in guidelines with a compass. If your design reveals the centre, you will have to do some angled cuts as you approach the middle. To minimize the need for these, make the centrepiece larger – using a whole tile if the rest is in quarters, or four tiles cut to a circle (fig. 6).

STREAKS

One way to change colour in the background is to stagger the change on alternating rows, creating interlocking 'fingers' of colour. This allows a gradual transition and avoids a distracting dividing line (fig. 7).

WAVES

You can introduce more curves into the background by widening and narrowing certain lines in a wave-like pattern. This can also be a way of introducing lines of different colours (fig. 8).

ANIMAL PANELS

This series of designs explores different ways of laying quarter-cut glass mosaic. In each case, the object was to experiment with the relationship between foreground and background, demonstrating the harmony between them without letting the animals disappear altogether. The overall effect is of a flat, evenly patterned surface in the midst of which, with varying degrees of clarity, lurks a strange animal.

METHOD TIPS

These panels could be made either as a complete set or as individual pieces. Their use of colour is quite complicated and would require some previous experience of working with mosaic. The designs can be made as framed panels to hang on a wall or incorporated into a larger area of wall mosaic. For instance, a single animal could be used to make a centrepiece for a wash basin splashback or the complete set could run around a bath.

• Both the direct and the indirect method of mosaic are suitable for these projects (see pages 112 and 114). If you are making your own design and experimenting with colour and pattern, the indirect method is recommended because it is easier to make adjustments as you work. Equally, if you are intending to fix the mosaic to a vertical surface, it is more comfortable to make the piece on a horizontal surface using the indirect method. However, if you are making a mosaic panel and following a design that has already been worked out, the direct method would also be suitable.

• The first step to creating the mosaic is to draw the design on to either paper or board, depending on your chosen method. You need

only show the main lines of the design (see Templates, p136) as the subsidiary lines of laying will follow on automatically. Seeing the project drawn to full size will make it easier to estimate the quantities of different colours you will need.

• The size of the animal panels is approximately 46 x 45cm (18½ x 18in). If you are going to set them into other tiles or sheets of mosaic you could amend the dimensions slightly to fit, although a dramatic change in the overall size will make it difficult to follow the way in which the tiles have been laid.

• Before starting to lay the tiles, avoid the need for final adjustments by spending some time working out which colours you will use in all the different areas. When you have chosen your colours, cut a small quantity of quarter-tiles.

• To work these panels, start with the animal and then fill in the background. When making either animals or figures it is best to start with the face or head as this will give the piece immediate focus and character.

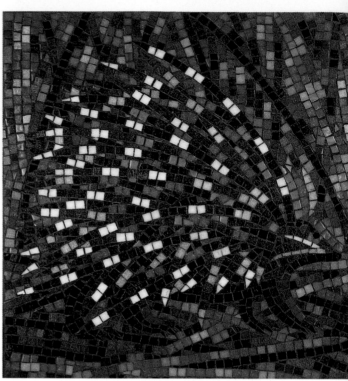

ANTEATER

At first sight the anteater seems a difficult subject for mosaic as its coat has no obvious pattern or texture. However, in silhouette, the line of the back, neck and head forms a graceful curve which has been used as a basis for the rolling hills and overhanging tree.

Within these flat bands of colour, flecks of gradated tones have been set to give a subtle indication of curving form. The even distribution of these flecks gives the piece an overall cohesion by setting up a regular rhythm across both the anteater and the background. It is important that the 'spots' are evenly spaced; if not the eye would be immediately drawn to that area and an imbalance created in the piece.

The gentle curves of the design can be easily followed with square pieces and there is relatively little cutting involved, with the effects relying largely on colour changes and lines of laying.

PORCUPINE

Although made up of a series of straight lines, the porcupine is the most difficult mosaic to make. The angle at which the quills project from the body give the animal its shape, but because they splay out and cross over one another there is a lot of cutting involved. The bright white points were introduced to attract the eye and give shape to the mass of needles, which would otherwise look confusing. These points are echoed in the background by the use of the lighter colours in the grasses, which stand out equally strongly but help to differentiate the animal in its surroundings.

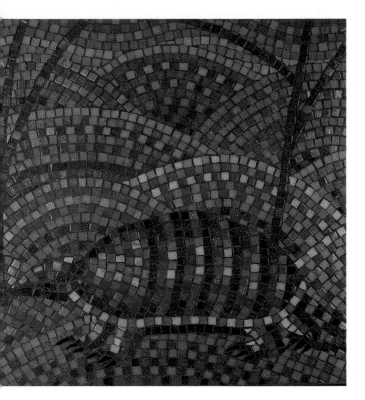

ARMADILLO

With its sectional divisions, the shell of an armadillo is an ideal subject for mosaic as it is naturally conveyed as a pattern of lines and spots. This idea has been applied to the rounded hills of the landscape, which also relate to the traditional fan pattern.

The armadillo is distinguished from the background in three ways. First, the shell is laid in a different direction from the hills behind. Second, a different colour combination has been used on the armadillo, although all the individual colours occur elsewhere in the piece. Third, shades of dark and light have been used to give the shell form, being darker at the edges than in the middle. The hills, in contrast, are darker towards the bottom, emphasizing the fact that they lie one in front of the other.

PANGOLIN

The pangolin is a creature covered in large scales that lives on the floor of tropical forests. The scales are similar in shape to the leaves and the design treats the two elements in a suitably related way. The tight curves necessarily require a lot of cutting and care to keep them neat and elegant. To make the rounded shape, the inner row needs to be laid to a point to reduce cutting, but the outer row must be laid around the curve with angled cuts as necessary.

RHINOCEROS

This panel is made of quarter-cut unglazed ceramic tiles. The animal is described by a series of lines of mosaic which reflect both the folds and wrinkles in its hide and the contours of its shape. The palette is restricted to only a few colours and they are arranged tonally, with the darkest colour delineating the underside and rear and the palest used on the head, horn, ears and light folds on the body. Instead of using tonal gradations of the same colour, the piece features deliberate variations between browns, greys and blues to make combinations that are interesting in themselves as well as conveying the leathery quality of the rhino's hide.

In clear contrast to the previous panels the rhinoceros stands against a completely plain, off-white background. This is an effect commonly used in Roman floor mosaics where decorative elements and pictorial motifs are often set floating in a sea of plain marble.

METHOD TIPS

Made of unglazed ceramic tiles, this piece would be suitable for setting into a floor or, as the material is hard-wearing and frost-proof, for use on a garden path or terrace. The project does require a lot of quarter-cutting, but it is a simple design to follow and is ideal for beginners.

• Floor mosaics need to be as flat as possible, both to prevent damage, and to make them easy to keep clean. For this reason the indirect method (see p114) is recommended.

• The piece measures 60 × 60cm (24 × 24in) and if you are setting it into thicker tiles you could fix it to a board to make a panel of compatible depth. In wet areas or outdoors the board should be of mineral composition and not sensitive to moisture. To make the project fit your own available space, simply change the amount of background area in the design.

• Start by drawing the rhinoceros on a piece of paper, giving yourself rough guidelines for the different coloured lines (see Template, p140).

The tiles will set up their own rhythm and flow and you should consider adjusting the lines instead of always embarking on special cutting.

• As with the other animal panels, start laying the design at the head. In a relatively simple piece like this the facial expression is very important. Once you have laid the tiles, it is easy to make minor cutting adjustments that will make a significant difference to the overall effect.

• When you come to the background, cut a quantity of quarter-tiles but do not be too careful as the more irregular the shapes, the better the effect will be. Do not try to lay to a predetermined line but let the accidental shapes of the tiles, combined with the outline of the animal, dictate a natural and flowing *andamenti*.

• If you are making an unframed panel, lay a straight row of tiles around the edge to form a mosaic frame. This will prevent any small cut tiles being laid around the edge and falling off — larger straight tiles will stand a better chance of staying in place.

FISH TABLE

The idea of the design was to produce a feeling of movement – in the swimming fish, the swirling reeds and the swaying background. The most critical decision was the positioning of the fish so that as well as expressing their individual movements, there is a sense of flow between them as if they are following an invisible current in the water. The curling lines of the weeds suggest unseen eddies while the gentler curves of the net are reminiscent of the distortion of straight lines seen underwater.

The fish themselves are made in quarter-cut tiles to give the detail required to make them lively. The tiles across the body are laid along the diagonal set up by a row of triangles laid along the spine. This gives an effect of scales which change colour along the fish's centre-line to the pale grey and white of the belly. It is partly because they are not a particular type of fish but a stylized expression of the idea of a fish in mosaic that the execution can be simple and strong enough to convey the twists and turns that give them their liveliness.

The half-cut tiles of the weeds suggest a rippling surface characteristic of some water plants. Again, the colours and shapes are not entirely naturalistic, but a distillation of an idea expressed in a simple but evocative form. The background is relatively plain, laid in whole tiles following the undulating lines of the net. The line chosen is always a parallel diagonal so the direction of the lines is always similar but not identical, as with waves rolling across shallows to the shore.

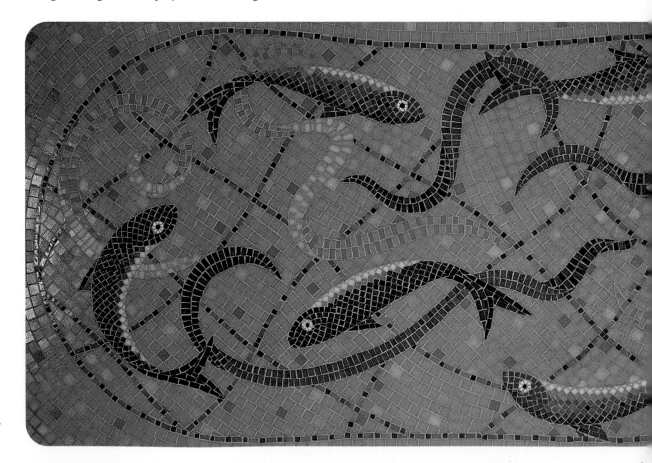

METHOD TIPS

This piece is designed as a tabletop and the indirect method should be used to ensure a flat surface (see page 114). The size of this project makes it more suitable for those with some experience of mosaic, but none of the techniques involved are complicated.

• When drawing out the design, remember that the flow of the lines is crucial to the illusion of movement. Try to keep the drawing simple but bold, using continuous lines wherever possible and concentrating on the grace and flow of the lines rather than on their exact accuracy to the original.

• Start the piece by making the fish. Their lines of laying are generated by the row of triangles along their backbone. Having set up the diagonals across the body, move on to the head which should be completed simply, laying tiles of a single colour around the eye with as little cutting as possible.

• With a piece this size (240 × 83.5cm/96 × 33½in), you will need to cut it up into sections before fixing. Using a sharp stanley knife, divide the piece following lines in the design whenever possible – along the lines of the net, for example. This will make cutting easier and will also make the joints between sections invisible when fixed.

• Each section should be of a manageable size to turn over and fix, generally a maximum of 50 × 50cm (20 × 20in). Reassemble the piece face up on the floor and then number the sections, adding an arrow on each to indicate the direction of laying. Mark this on a diagram which can then be followed when fixing the piece in its final location.

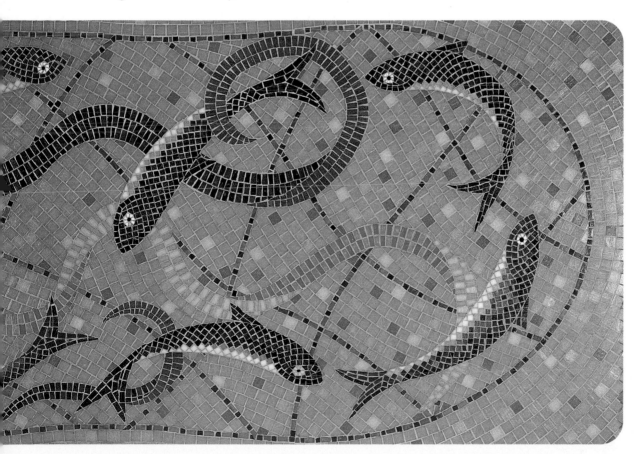

GALLERY

PISCES

This mosaic was commissioned by a client whose star sign provided a suitable decorative feature for his swimming pool. The large fish are laid simply along a gentle curve, which emphasizes the form of their bodies. As it is a circular panel, the background is laid to the circumference which echoes the composition of the fish circling around each other.

When designing mosaics to be seen underwater do take into consideration the effects that reflection from the water surface will have on the piece. The movement of the water will add to the animation of the design but it is important that the execution is bold and contains high contrast so that it will still read clearly under water.

Another property of water to consider is the way in which the side walls of a pool appear to shrink to a fraction of their real size. This makes them unsuitable areas for decoration as a design would be distorted beyond recognition.

PIGS

These saddlebacks are one of a pair of panels commissioned to decorate an old piggery, sadly no longer occupied by pigs. The pigs' bodies have been laid in two different ways to express their form. The dark rear end is laid to the rounded contour of the pig's belly, while the pale front and snout are laid to the expressive curving line of the profile. Interesting lines, such as the line of the lower pig's ears, are emphasized by being chosen as the line of laying.

The client particularly requested that the pigs be set against a dark background to give the illusion of looking into the building with the animals inside. As the pigs are themselves dark in places, it was important to introduce a range of tones that could be used to make the animals read clearly against the background, with dark against light and light against dark. These colours are blended by 'fingering' together, softening the colour transition so that the effect does not dominate the foreground.

SUNFLOWER TABLE

This table was made for a client's garden. The sunflower is a common motif in the history of English decorative arts, and was particularly associated with the Arts and Crafts movement. Here it is interpreted in a contemporary way, being enlarged to fill the entire tabletop. The whole piece is laid in the same way, using randomly cut triangles and irregular halves, placed to interlock like crazy paving. This is a very simple technique to use, requiring no skilled cutting and yet creating a lively overall effect. However, it is important to keep the gaps between the tiles more or less even as this will give the piece a sense of order and harmony.

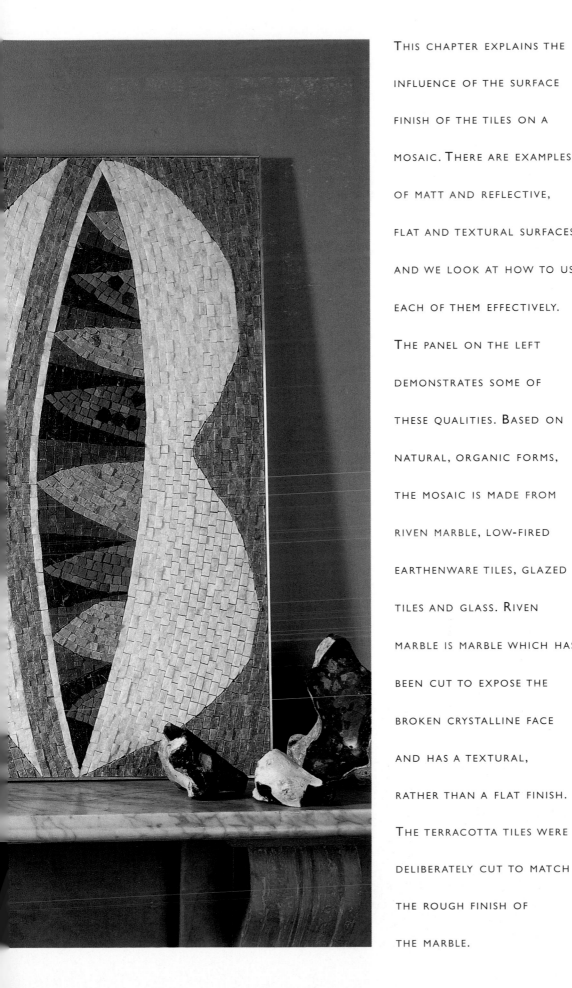

THIS CHAPTER EXPLAINS THE
INFLUENCE OF THE SURFACE
FINISH OF THE TILES ON A
MOSAIC. THERE ARE EXAMPLES
OF MATT AND REFLECTIVE,
FLAT AND TEXTURAL SURFACES,
AND WE LOOK AT HOW TO USE
EACH OF THEM EFFECTIVELY.
THE PANEL ON THE LEFT
DEMONSTRATES SOME OF
THESE QUALITIES. BASED ON
NATURAL, ORGANIC FORMS,
THE MOSAIC IS MADE FROM
RIVEN MARBLE, LOW-FIRED
EARTHENWARE TILES, GLAZED
TILES AND GLASS. RIVEN
MARBLE IS MARBLE WHICH HAS
BEEN CUT TO EXPOSE THE
BROKEN CRYSTALLINE FACE
AND HAS A TEXTURAL,
RATHER THAN A FLAT FINISH.
THE TERRACOTTA TILES WERE
DELIBERATELY CUT TO MATCH
THE ROUGH FINISH OF
THE MARBLE.

5 SURFACE

REFLECTIVE MOSAICS

Some mosaic materials, such as smalti, gold and silver, are intensely reflective. They have long been used for their symbolic and aesthetic qualities, particularly in churches and mosques, although today, gold and silver tend to be used sparingly as they are expensive and can be hard to use. If it is laid roughly, gold has a kind of predictable reflectivity, but laid very flat it does not always reflect light and can look rather muted. Silver can behave in a similar way, looking grey and unimpressive. To make the most of the material angle all the tiles slightly as you fix them. You will be amazed at the difference it makes to the way they catch the light.

The reverse face of silver and gold is rich and beautiful. It is often coloured blue or green, although you can sometimes find tiles backed with a whole range of colours, from yellow or pink to brilliant green. Pavimento tiles are less rare. They are silver or gold, covered in transparent glass, and can be seen

THESE POLISHED MARBLE CUBES ALL HAVE A GLASSY FINISH. IT CAN BE EFFECTIVE TO CONTRAST MATT AND POLISHED TILES.

in the marble garden pavement at the beginning of Chapter 3, Contrast (see page 36). They have a certain degree of reflectivity, but more importantly they give a sense of depth. Use them carefully as they can seem rather pointless scattered about a design which does not make sense of them.

Mirror is another reflective material which is sometimes combined with mosaic. Its contrasting surfaces are interesting but difficult to use well. Mirror introduces a new element to mosaic, bringing a reflection of the outside world into a static mosaic. Helping to draw attention to a surface is arguably mirror's most useful role.

Mirror can also work well used on its own and whole areas of broken mirror can look very attractive. Mirror has an integrity which is lost when it is combined with other materials, probably because the way you read a reflective surface is not the same as the way you understand an unreflective one. The combination, unless carefully structured, can be very confusing. The busy jazziness of the reflective surface makes it hard to read shapes that are combined with it.

SILVER, GOLD AND THEIR REVERSE FACE IN GREEN AND BLUE GLASS ARE COMBINED HERE WITH BLACK RIVEN MARBLE.

TEXTURAL MOSAICS

HERE RIVEN MARBLE IS COMBINED WITH CUT CERAMIC LAID ON ITS SIDE, THE SIMILARITIES OF THEIR SURFACE PROPERTIES ADDING INTEREST TO THE CONTRAST.

Like reflective mosaics, textural mosaics are not easy to do well. The most commonly used mosaic tile with texture is smalti. Smalti is tricky to use for reasons which are more to do with intensity than with texture. In fact, it is the textural properties of smalti that hint at how to use it effectively. The curved and broken glassy face attracts and throws light, providing a flickery, interesting surface.

The history of mosaic is not exactly littered with mosaics that show an interest in texture. Where such pieces exist, they are generally as a consequence of an interest in something else, perhaps colour or reflectivity. Texture is a 20th-century preoccupation and, like contrast, it probably comes from the modernist philosophy of truth to materials. This idea suggests that every material must display itself as an essential distillation of its own nature. In the case of texture, where silver is used, it is not only reflective, but it stands for reflectivity. Materials are both themselves and symbolic of themselves.

This idea is itself a discipline, and is helpful when attempting to use a variety of textures. Look at the material you plan to use and decide what it tells you about anything else you want to use with it. Does it relate in terms of colour, surface or tone? Perhaps the shape of it suggests a specific treatment? Think carefully before introducing a lot of differing elements. The fact that one material varies from another is not a good enough reason for including it. An unsophisticated, but widely held approach to colour is to use one because it is different to another, rather than for any relationship it has with the other. Make sure you are not approaching texture with the same attitude. It is also artificial to talk about texture as if it could be isolated from the material which bears it. The textural material has its own qualities, for example colour. If you want the focus of interest to be the texture, you need to limit the range of these other qualities.

THE FRACTURED FACE OF SMALTI CONTRASTS WITH RIVEN MARBLE. THE LIGHT-ABSORBENT MARBLE AND LIGHT-REFLECTIVE GLASS MAKE THIS AN EFFECTIVE COMBINATION.

SMALTI & MARBLE PANEL

This simple panel shows a plant made from smalti against a marble background. The background is used for its matt crystalline surface, which contrasts with the glassy, reflective face of smalti. Both materials are cut to the same rectangular shape to create a visual relationship between the contrasting surface treatments.

The design is given structure, and another kind of reflective treatment, by using bands of painted silver which help to give a sense of depth. The simplicity of the design demonstrates a series of lessons. First, there is no need for symmetry for a design to work. Next, there is no need for a motif which is the focus of visual interest to be placed centrally. Finally, larger areas of dark colour can be used at the top of a design without the bottom seeming to be overshadowed. You do not have to worry too much about realism for it to be clear what a design is depicting; nor is it necessary to use naturalistic colour.

METHOD TIPS

This design is fairly simple and can be attempted by a beginner using the direct method (see page 112).

• Start with significant features, in this case the plant and berries. Make sure you balance the colour in your mosaic. In this design, larger areas of dark colour appear at the top than at the bottom. This works here because other elements in the design are in balance with one another. The fact that all the stems meet centrally at the bottom draws the eye to that point and gives it emphasis. So a focus point can help to balance a colour. Pattern can also help to balance intensity.

• Do not feel that you have to make your design symmetrical. You can place an object in the middle of a design, but it is likely to be more interesting, in that it is less immediately obvious what it is doing, if you do not. If your design balances in a more complex way than symmetry, it appears more interesting to the onlooker. Symmetry and centrality are used for good reasons: they provide shortcuts to making a design harmonious, and a good design certainly needs a sense of order and harmony. But discovering how to do this without recourse to a formula will ultimately create a much more satisfying design.

UNGROUTED GLASS MIRROR

This mirror is made from quarter-cut vitreous glass. It has a shimmery and luminous finished surface which comes from two sources. The fish bodies are shaded tonally, which helps them to look scaly and interesting: in one the effect lies in the tonal variation of the colours used; in the other it is the fact that the mosaic has been left ungrouted. Grout has a very unifying effect on mosaic. Leaving a mosaic ungrouted allows colours to work directly in relation to one another. Grout can have a very desirable quality of drawing all the colours together, but if a mosaic uses a range of hues and tones, it can also mute or fracture colour relationships. Making a mosaic without grouting it can give you a fresh outlook on a palette of colours. It enables you to use high contrast without worrying about what this will do to the balance of the piece once the mosaic has been grouted

This mirror uses the tiles in the conventional way, stuck down with their textural face to the the board. It is possible, however, and technically easier, to stick the flat face to the board and use the mosaic for its textured side. This face has a different way of reflecting the light. Some mosaic tiles have a different quality of colour on their reverse than they have on their flat face. Try working with them: it will certainly extend the creative range of what you can do in mosaic.

METHOD TIPS

This design involves cutting accurate quarter-tiles and this requires a high level of skill and experience. The mirror should be made using the direct method (see page 112).

• To reproduce the shimmery quality of the bodies of the fish, you need to butt the tiles closely together. This means having to cut quite accurately so as to maintain the linear sense of the scales.

• Ungrouted mosaic is probably best made by sticking it directly to the board. Where the tiles are placed close together you must take care not to let glue squeeze up between the joints and foul the surface of the tiles. Having no grout means you cannot rely on any other element to draw areas of colour together. Keep checking to see that the image is sufficiently clear and change your tile selection if it seems to be losing definition.

• Sticking directly to the board rather than working in reverse allows you to angle the tiles slightly as you lay them on the board. Make creative use of the light-reflective properties of these tiles as part of your design.

GOLD & SILVER PANEL

This panel combines five kinds of surface treatments; reflective gold and silver, the reverse face of these to introduce a sense of depth, matt vitreous glass, shiny vitreous glass, and gemme, which is glass saturated with metallic ore. This is a tricky combination to keep in balance and the design is structured to build up to areas of hotter colour, or more intensely reflective surface. The idea for this design came from an embroidered cushion. Textiles are often a rich source of inspiration for a mosaicist. Early Coptic weaving shows the influence of mosaic. Many carpets share border designs with mosaic, which is not really surprising as both disciplines rely on a unit – a stitch or a tile – and a module or repeat. Both rugs and mosaics are used on floors, as a practical and decorative way of dividing up areas and giving clues about the function and importance of the space they inhabit.

Take time to look at textiles, as they are a rich decorative resource. Even something like whitework, which is a type of embroidery where you use white threads on a white ground, has something to teach the mosaicist. Indian textiles are also very inspiring, both for the use of colour and the fascination with reflective surfaces. Once you start to see the decorative possibilities of the grout joints, you can begin to grasp the range of effects you can achieve in just one colour.

METHOD TIPS

This panel is made using vitreous glass, gemme (vitreous glass striated with metallic ore) and gold and silver tiles. The latter are expensive, but the design allows the material to be laid in quite a free way. Precise accuracy in cutting gold and silver is not required.

• This project is less successful than it might have been, as it was made using the indirect method (see page 114) and you should learn from this mistake. The piece contains a lot of gemme (metallic vitreous glass), which differs from one side to the other, and the browns and purples are not only different in the degree of metallic ore, but also vary in tone from one side to the other. The gold and silver (the reverse face of which is the blue and green used as decorative circles) is also reversed. With the indirect method, you cannot see the effect you are creating as you work and the direct method would have given more control (see page 112).

• The reds and oranges are crucial to this design. To achieve a sense of glowing colour, the tiles need to be cut and laid so they build in intensity. Work out a tonal gradation before starting to stick them down.

• Because the front and reverse of the tiles are different, the design is more chaotically arranged than intended. If the areas of figured glass had been less haphazardly placed, the piece would have been more successful. The materials are used largely to demonstrate the nature of their surfaces. As a rule, where materials are used with a greater degree of compositional structure, a design works better than where they are mixed more randomly.

GALLERY

ROAD TO DAMASCUS

This mosaic is a memento of a walk along a road in Syria that led to Damascus. A series of objects – broken tiles, pieces of brightly coloured bicycle reflector, bottle glass, a decorative beer-bottle top and other small found items were collected for their interesting textures, shapes and surfaces and later made into a mosaic panel. The wobbly shaped frame echoes the random shapes of the tiles. The woodgrain on the frame has something in common with the blotchy surface of the tiles on the right. The items are structured so that the mid-toned items fuse together as a background, united in colour by the grout, and the more strongly coloured objects which are fractured by the grout form the central backbone of the design.

SLATE MIRROR

This mosaic mirror surround uses slate, vitreous glass mosaic, silver and broken glass. The grey slate has a slight purply sheen, and had little bits of grey-green lichen growing on it when it was found. These colours are all picked up by the vitreous glass which surrounds the slate and is combined with shiny and reflective material, intended to suggest the fissures you sometimes find between rocks. Although there is no continuity of shape between the pieces used, there is a continuity of relative flatness. The mosaic is textural, but it has more to do with surfaces. There is an overall balance between depth and reflectivity. The transparency of glass gives a sense of depth, taking light to a lower plane than the rest of the mosaic, where the silver reflects light back at you. The colour range is limited, and the idea of the design is a simple opposition between matt and shiny. Using reflective material around a mirror can work well, as it relates the mirror itself to its surrounding border.

CONES

This mosaic has two main areas of interest – surface and balance. The textural surface does the same thing across the whole design. Marble cubes have been cut and used for their riven face to echo the shape of smalti. The design is divided into two halves. One half shows an intensely coloured pair of cones, while the other is divided into two sets of cones, one on top of another. This shape is potentially clumsy and weighty and could easily become overbearing. The mosaic is really an exercise in making these two sides balance. The complex shapes on one side are balanced by the brightness of colour on the other. The intense shininess of the red and orange smalti is counterweighted by the light-absorbent, black marble. The lively linear top to the orange cone is balanced by the pattern of white and grey marble which runs in a band across the centre of the more complex form.

Try exercises like this for yourself. The issues you have to deal with are wide and various, so, to begin with, it is probably a good idea to limit yourself to a small range of materials and colours.

6 PATTERN

PATTERN IS INTEGRAL TO EVERY MOSAIC. ANY IMAGE MADE THIS WAY IS BUILT UP FROM A SERIES OF FRACTURED ELEMENTS, MAKING PATTERN AN INEVITABLE RESULT OF THE CREATIVE PROCESS. PATTERN IS A VERSATILE AND EXCITING ELEMENT OF MOSAIC AND THIS CHAPTER EXPLORES A VARIETY OF WAYS TO USE IT. THE PIECE SHOWN HERE, FOR EXAMPLE, IS ENTIRELY ABOUT PATTERN AND COLOUR AND REFERS TO THE TYPES OF DISTORTIONS AND COLOUR VARIATIONS SEEN IN WOVEN TEXTILES. ALTHOUGH IT IS NOT SYMMETRICAL, PATTERN EMERGES FROM THE REPETITION OF FORMS, COLOURS AND SHAPES. WITH NO FORMULA FOR THE WAY THE PATTERN IS LAID, CARE HAS BEEN TAKEN TO ENSURE THAT THE SHAPES, TONES AND COLOURS BALANCE THROUGHOUT.

USING PATTERN

Any mosaic is built up from a series of repeating shapes which create a pattern. By structuring the way these repeat you can create further patterns. These do not need to be symmetrical or completely regular, as pattern can emerge simply by repeating any element – a combination of colours for example. Pattern can be the principal theme of a mosaic, as it is in most of the items in this chapter. But it can also be subsidiary to the main theme – the way in which a background or border might be laid for example, or the pattern made by something depicted in a mosaic.

FOREGROUND PATTERN

This is pattern displayed by the principal feature of the mosaic. Look at the rhinoceros on page 56. The background has been laid in a way which follows the form of the animal and the shapes this makes have a rhythm of their own; but the folds on the rhinoceros's hide create contrasting patterns.

It is not unusual for the main feature of a mosaic to create more than one pattern. An example of this might be the pattern that drapery makes, as well as the pattern on the drapery. A complex image, like a person, will display a whole series of patterns. Every time you change the direction the tiles are laid, you produce a new one.

You can also use pattern to make visual jokes and references. Imagine that your mosaic is a traditional subject – a basket of fish. You could use the spots and stripes of the scaly fish bodies in a more muted way in the background, or make the woven form of the basket the pattern which forms the remaining field.

PATTERN AS A POINT OF FOCUS

Pattern can be used as the main feature of a mosaic, for example as a single decorative item surrounded by a border or a series of borders. Where a whole floor is treated with a single decorative idea, the results can be impressive.

When you are making a mosaic which is principally about pattern, bear in mind that pattern itself produces a sense of weight. This is something to consider when making a mosaic balance. Pattern in one area does not necessarily need to be balanced by pattern in another; you can use colour, reflection or an entirely different property to balance it. But you do need to take it into account. One pattern can, of course, be balanced by another. The mosaic on the fireplace (see page 74) shows how this can work. Panels C and D show how you can increase the sophistication of a simple pattern through complex colour.

BACKGROUND PATTERN

Pattern can be used in the background or field of a mosaic in a series of ways. Terms such as fan, or Opus Vermiculatum (meaning worm-like work) describe some of the more common patterns used to lay backgrounds and there is more information about these in Chapter 4, but it is also perfectly possible to invent your own patterning treatments. Look at panel A. Here the background is simple, straight-laid mosaic tiles and the foreground image is the pair of diamonds. Panel B shows the same piece with another shape on top of both foreground and background. This is a pattern created by overlaying shapes. For further

REPEATING A SHAPE LIKE THIS PAIR OF DIAMONDS IS
THE SIMPLEST WAY OF CREATING A PATTERN.

PATTERNS COME FROM ESTABLISHING A RULE AND
STICKING TO IT. HERE, BANDS OF COLOUR CHANGE
TONE FROM FOREGROUND TO BACKGROUND.

BY OVERLAYING SHAPES A MORE COMPLEX PATTERN IS
CREATED FROM A SIMPLE IDEA.

THROUGH STRUCTURING THE ARRANGEMENT OF
BACKGROUND COLOURS, OR USING THEM RANDOMLY,
AS HERE, FURTHER PATTERNS ARE CREATED.

examples see the mirrors on pages 84-85.

Imagine you wish to lay a background in
a single colour. This might seem limited until
you start to think about the range of effects
available. You can subdivide a single area into
a series of patterns and forms made by the
way in which the tiles are laid, you can cut the
tiles into different shapes, or you can
combine materials to give a variety of
reflective surfaces. Opportunities to create
pattern are seemingly endless before you even
begin to introduce further colours.

TARTAN TABLETOP

This tabletop shows the immensely sophisticated effects you can produce from the simplest of formulae. The rule here is a basic contrast of a box of four tiles of yellow, orange or green, against a dividing line of greeny-blue. The colours in the boxes are randomly but evenly interspersed. The interest of the piece comes from the wide variety of tonal colour, which makes it seem flickery and complex. The piece bears examination, because although the idea behind it is simple, it has been made in a way that the eye does not immediately grasp. The complexity of the tonal colour compels you to look at it for longer than you otherwise would, in order to understand it. The mosaic demonstrates the truth of the idea about successful design discussed in Chapter 5, Surface – variation in one area, restraint in another.

METHOD TIPS

Although this is a sophisticated design, it involves no cutting and would be suitable for a beginner. Part of its appeal comes from the absolute equality of colour intensity of the different hues. They are all related to one another, so much so that it is only on close examination that you notice how, in a couple of the boxes, they are combined.

• The tiles in this design are used whole, and simply soaked off the pre-laid sheets. To make a design like this successfully, draw a grid on to a piece of paper, making sure that it is large enough for both the tiles and grout joints. This will be the actual surface used to take the tiles, and even though the design is extremely simple, it is a good idea to mark the location of the boxes of four tiles, as mistakes are surprisingly easy to make.

• You will not manage to reproduce a design which has the flickery tonal interest of this piece unless you choose your colours from a range of tiles. If you make the piece from four colours alone you will find the results rather static in comparison. Make a selection of tiles, and choose a range which is as tonally close as possible. If you are unable to find precisely these hues, remember the principles that make this design work and you will be able to substitute others effectively.

• This mosaic was made using the indirect method (see page 114). It was grouted in grey which was the least intrusive, and the closest in tone to the tiles. If you use different colours from the ones shown here, remember to select a grout closest in tone to the field colour.

CERAMIC TABLE

This mosaic tabletop was made to demonstrate the point that every gap between the tiles has expressive possibilities. It is up to you to decide how you want to make these spaces work, and what you want them to say. The colours used in the mosaic are limited to allow the grout joints to be the main focus of attention. Within these tight constraints, the tiles were cut and laid in as many ways as possible. There is no absolute rule about the size of the gap you leave between tiles, but the effect is most pleasing if it is consistent across the whole piece. Because this tabletop relies on this spacing to produce its lace-like patterns, the gap left is fairly wide.

METHOD TIPS

This design involves a certain degree of skill in cutting and laying and so is not ideal for a beginner. Though it uses a limited colour range, there are a variety of tile shapes. The broad contrast between different cuts makes it necessary to find a design that structures and makes sense of them. Dividing the circle up into areas means that each section can contain a pattern, while the overall structure gives the design coherence at the same time.

• Use the differing surface qualities of materials as part of the pattern. This tabletop combines unglazed ceramic and vitreous glass. The contrast of matt and reflective surfaces and differing tones of white lend the piece added interest and life.

• Nothing gives a colour emphasis more than contrasting it with another. To make the mosaic look really white and fractured, lay an area of blue-grey mosaic around the edge. Whereas the grey grout breaks up the white tiles, it unites this background. Cut it in a crazy way to maintain some similarity with the white, and use a mix of materials including vitreous glass and an even more reflective glazed ceramic tile.

• This mosaic was made on paper using the indirect method (see page 114). With experimental pieces like this, it is very useful to be able to work indirect, as no decision needs to be absolutely final until the piece is fixed. It is therefore always possible to decide that one or other area is not working as well as you might wish, and to soak it off the paper from the back.

BORDERS

These borders treat an identical design in a number of ways. The aim of this was to show how even the simplest theme can be made to seem surprisingly rich through the way in which the cuts and colours are arranged.

METHOD TIPS

• The border below has been made in unglazed ceramic. The colours used here and also in the vitreous glass border (bottom right) are similar so that the differences in the nature of the materials show up clearly. The tessarae in this piece are laid in a haphazard way, sometimes known as Opus Palladianum. You will notice that the tone of the grout is very similar to the tone of the blue and green tiles. It has one unfortunate effect – the form of the leaf shapes has become unclear. The close tones and the all-over effect of the laying method do not give the skeletal impression of the structure that a more conventional way of laying tiles can produce.

• The border opposite demonstrates that you do not need strong or contrasting colour to give a shape definition. Treat the fracturing of the grout lines and the laying of the tiles as if they were pencil marks on paper. They help describe the form through line. Although the white and cream unglazed ceramic are tonally close, this border has better definition than that below which uses contrasting colour. The background is made with Opus Palladianum and the leaf shapes are more conventionally quartered tiles.

• The third border is made with vitreous glass. Close tones have been used in both the leaves and the background. This helps to give a soft, subtle appearance to the design. Although the colour of the tiles resembles those used in the unglazed ceramic border, the mosaic has a reflective glossy surface rather than a matt one similar to the grout.

UNGLAZED CERAMIC

UNGLAZED CERAMIC

VITREOUS GLASS

GALLERY

SQUARE AND CIRCULAR MIRRORS

Like the borders, these two mirrors demonstrate how a single idea can be interpreted in a variety of colours and to different effect. The simple idea behind these mirrors is to subdivide a space and fill the different areas with various patterns. These mirrors are given complexity by slightly breaking the rule. If the rule of tonal variation

was adhered to rigidly, and the thin band of colour running through the mosaic was always lighter than the rest, the result would probably be less interesting. The fact that the rule is sometimes broken makes it less immediately easy to grasp what is going on, with the consequence that the mosaic calls for closer examination.

The circular mirror uses the same system as the square mirror, with the difference that the band of tonal variation grows wider and narrower around the border. Care has been taken to ensure the bright, dark and intense colours balance around the circle. Lime green and bright red are an unusual colour combination, but in this context they have been made to work well.

PAVING SLABS

This path is made from a series of simple, cast slabs. Casting is enjoyable and rewarding, and it is also a perfect vehicle for a series of experiments, as none of them take too long to make. The slabs are really best used in the garden, however, as they are thick and heavy.

You can maintain immense freedom with a piece like this. It does not really matter if some of the tiles are extremely simple, as the effect is created by a whole series of them. In fact, it is probably better if some of them are simple; they do not all need to be busy. This path is made from black and white tiles, but you could equally well use colour. The tesserae in most of these tiles have not been very adventurously cut, but if you want to experiment with a variety of patterns and cutting techniques, a project like this is an ideal place to start.

TRADITIONALLY MOSAIC HAS
OFTEN BEEN USED AS A MEDIUM
TO DEPICT THE HUMAN FACE
AND FIGURE. LIVELY AND
ANIMATED EFFECTS CAN
BE CREATED THROUGH THE
CAREFUL USE OF LINES OF
LAYING AND TECHNIQUES OF
SHADING. IN THE 'COSMONAUT
PANEL' ILLUSTRATED, THE
FIGURES ARE EXECUTED IN THE
TRADITIONAL MATERIAL, SMALTI,
BUT ARE HIGHLY STYLIZED IN
TREATMENT. THE COMPOSITION
IS OF CRUCIAL IMPORTANCE TO
THE PIECE, WITH THE FIGURES
POSITIONED TO GIVE A SENSE
OF WEIGHTLESSNESS, AS IF THEY
ARE FLOATING IN SPACE. THIS
CHAPTER WILL LOOK AT WAYS
OF CREATING THE ILLUSION
OF FORM AND SELECTING AN
INTERESTING COLOUR PALETTE,
AS WELL AS THE CHALLENGES OF
HUMAN FIGURE COMPOSITION.

7

FACES & FIGURES

HUMAN FIGURE COMPOSITION

The interpretation of the figure in different times is influenced by styles adopted in other media, such as painting and sculpture (see Chapter 8). These historical styles demonstrate the priorities given to different aspects of the figure, such as movement versus stillness, and realism versus intensity, and represent general design decisions to be considered in any depiction of the human figure.

MOVEMENT

It is a good idea to start with the position and pose of the figures themselves. One of the attractions of the human body as a subject is its extreme flexibility – all its different components can be precisely manipulated into the composition that you require.

Composition will be dictated both by the shape of the available space and by the subject's expressive meaning. If you are conveying a particular kind of movement, such as swimming, you need to find the one position that best conveys the movement's cycle. This concentration of effect helps to create intensity in an image and can be extended beyond the boundaries of realism to create stylized, yet evocative forms. Not all figurative pieces convey movement. Some of the most magnificent mosaics ever produced, the great Byzantine and medieval church mosaics, derive their power from the expression of an intense stillness.

PROPORTION

Another consideration in the design of mosaic figures is proportion. The eye is especially sensitive to the human face and figure, differentiating between individuals instantly and without conscious thought. Tiny variations that would go unnoticed anywhere else, such as on the bark of a tree, are of important significance in the human face. Equally, the eye picks up any distortions in the human figure that seem unnatural, such as outsized heads or unequal limbs. This is not to say that distortion cannot be used to positive effect. The great Byzantine figures have very large eyes, and artists such as El Greco and Giacometti have used elongation to create distinctive and powerful figures.

TONE

Strong and simple figures can be described as outlines or flat shapes. More sophisticated effects, however, can be achieved using tone to suggest form. If you position an imaginary light source, you can then work out how the light would fall on different areas of the body. It is usually necessary to simplify the effect so that each element of the figure – limbs, torso and head – have a dark and a light side regardless of their exact position. The transition from dark to light across the surface will create the illusion of the curving form. Folds in clothes and drapery can be used to suggest the form of the body behind.

COLOUR

The choice of palette for the skin tones is very important. A wide range of flesh tones is available in smalti, but in vitreous glass and marble the range is far more restricted. Flesh is a strange colour and not always easy to combine attractively with other colours, but it contains hints of the entire spectrum. These can be exaggerated and colours of many different hues of the right tonal values can be used to enliven the image.

LAYING

The direction of the lines of laying are of crucial importance when translating your design into mosaic. When working across a complex shape like a face or figure, different lines will intercept each other and cuts at these junctions may set up unintentional, distracting lines. Therefore, junctions between directions and tones should, wherever possible, coincide with meaningful contours in the anatomy, for instance around the joints. Difficulties will arise particularly if you are laying parallel to the outline of the body and one way to avoid this is to outline the body and infill with crossing lines across the shapes from side to side. This will give the effect of curving contours and enhance the three-dimensional illusion.

LAYING PARALLEL: THE DIFFERENT TONES RUN PARALLEL TO THE OUTLINE OF THE FACE, WITH CHANGES IN DIRECTION COINCIDING WITH FEATURES.

LAYING ACROSS: THE LINES FOLLOW A CURVING LINE ACROSS THE FACE SET UP BY THE EYES AND EYEBROWS.

LINEAR: DIFFERENT TONES ARE USED TO PICK OUT PARTICULAR LINES AND THE AREAS BETWEEN ARE LAID IN STRAIGHT LINES.

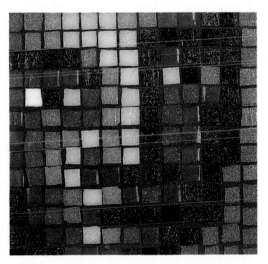

PIXELLATION: LAID ON A GRID DEFINITION OF THE FACE, FORM IS ACHIEVED THROUGH CHANGES IN TONE.

ASTRONAUT

This small panel depicts the stylized head of a spaceman. The overall treatment of the piece is very simple and derives its inspiration from the illumination of the planets by the sun. Thus on one side of the piece the face is dark, and on the other, it is light. To make the image balance, the background tones are also transposed so that there is not too great a disparity between the proportion of black to white on the two sides. The face is described using simple lines, but it is not identical on both sides. In design terms, while symmetry can be used to create idealized images, asymmetry often conveys character. Here, the eyes are at slightly different angles and the nose is described differently on the two sides.

To create these details, smaller cubes have been used in these lines and in parts of the helmet. The microphone is simply a circle cut from a single large cube and the infilling is executed in cubes of uniform size, adding unity to the piece. They are laid as simply as possible to avoid too many cuts or small pieces. The round helmet is emphasized by laying the cubes around the circumference, and these arcs are then echoed in the laying of the background. The radiating grout lines, combined with the tight fit of the image to its frame, add to the dynamism of the piece as if the astronaut is hurtling through space towards you.

Old marble cubes have been used and the slight variations in tone and size give the piece a livelier feel. Using recycled materials also creates an effect of instant antiquity, in this case in deliberate contrast to the subject matter. The panel has been grouted grey, as a mid tone between the black and white. This breaks up the two colours equally and helps to unify the whole.

METHOD TIPS

The piece measures 300 × 300mm (12x12in) and was made as a wall panel, but could equally well be set into a stone floor or cast as a paving slab (see page 122).

• The panel was made using the indirect method (see page 114). The cubes used are of varying thicknesses, and although the direct method (see page 112) could be used, it would result in a very uneven surface. Start by laying the square tiles around the border, leaving off one side so that you can sweep out the debris from cutting. Then lay the linear elements of the features and helmet, and finally fill in the remaining areas. Using the indirect method, a layer of adhesive can be spread across the back of the mosaic filling up the lower areas before placing it on the combed bed on the board. This is called 'buttering' the back and creates an adhesive bed of variable thickness and a relatively flat surface.

• If you have used this technique, one of the advantages of the level surface is that you will be able to 'hone' the mosaic. This involves rubbing down the unpolished marble with 'wet and dry' abrasive paper to produce a semi-polished appearance that intensifies the colours without giving a shiny surface. Marble is surprisingly soft, and a short period of hard rubbing with a sanding block (a piece of 'wet and dry' wrapped around a timber block) will produce encouraging results. This technique is also useful if you have used cubes with a polished face and want to bring down the extreme glossiness to a matt finish.

THE YELLOW TABLECLOTH

This panel, although very stylized, is primarily concerned with the creation of a three-dimensional illustration. It shows a figure standing in a room with a table and a bowl of fruit. All the surfaces are patterned, and the illusion of a figure in space is created entirely through the manipulation of light and dark tones. In ancient times the Hellenistic school of Roman mosaics created pictorial scenes with illusions of depth for the centrepieces of floor mosaics, as well as for wall panels such as those found at Pompeii. Since then, however, mosaics have developed with flatter and plainer backgrounds. This is partly because these worked better on floors where illusionism could be disorientating for the observer as it created a sense of depth below the plane of the floor itself. In the case of wall mosaics in the early Christian era, the emphasis of the designs was didactic and instructional, and plain, flat backgrounds helped to project their meaning outwards into the architectural space and then towards the audience. The tradition of creating an artificial space within the picture plane to draw in the viewer was subsequently taken up and pursued in the field of painting.

This panel owes as much to ideas taken from paintings as it does to mosaic itself. The subject of a figure in a room is one of the most common in Impressionist, Post-Impressionist and early modern paintings, being used by such painters as Degas and Matisse, while the juxtaposition of patterned surfaces is a device much used by Vuillard.

TONAL TRANSITION

METHOD TIPS

Creating an illusion in mosaic requires precise control over the tones of colours used – a skill that is acquired through experience. This piece is therefore suitable for more advanced mosaicists.

• This mosaic can be executed using the direct method (see page 112), but since the tonal transitions are difficult to achieve and might need adjustment, the indirect method is probably the most suitable (see page 114).

• With its many references to painting, this design is suitable for a framed panel to be hung on the wall. Frames can be made by pinning and gluing timber beading to the edge of the board. This is best done before fixing the mosaic to avoid the possibility of knocking off the edge pieces in the process. Flexible copper strips can also be used to frame the piece. Pin these to the board at 5cm (2in) intervals with copper hardboard pins. Alternatively, the design can be set into areas of plain tiling to form a 'virtual picture' on a bathroom or kitchen wall.

• The size of this panel is 96 x 47cm (38⅜ x 18¾in). Similar, although cruder, effects can be achieved on smaller panels. For this project it would be a good idea to set up the wall, ceiling and floor areas of the design first so that you can be sure that the tonal relationships are correct, and also that the figure, lampshade and table will read clearly against them.

PATTERN

This indicates the play of light through subtle changes in tone in individual spots across a plain field.

TONAL GRADATION

The most realistic rendition of form depends on having a large palette of colour.

LINEAR TRANSITIONS

This avoids the need to set up a distracting vertical line at the change of colour.

SEQUENTIAL GRADATION

This is a technique for gradually blending from one colour to another without using tiles of intermediate tones.

ANGEL

This project is made with smalti, the Venetian enamelled glass traditionally used in Roman, Byzantine and medieval mosaics. Smalti is a material of great intensity. It works very well in large architectural spaces and when seen from a great distance. It is thus particularly suitable for church work. It can also be used for relatively small panels such as this one (100 x 80cm/40 x 32in). As the effect of the mosaic is very strong, the panel needs to be hung on its own wall with plenty of space around it otherwise it will overpower anything placed close by.

The design of the panel was generated by the idea that the composition of the figure should fill, as far as possible, the whole panel. This kind of tight fit to the outer edges is common in medieval stone and wood carving where much ingenuity is exercised to make all kinds of creatures, figures and faces fit into the fixed sizes of bosses and capitals. Within these constraints, the aim was to convey a sense that the angel was flying through the air.

Because of the intensity of the smalti there is a very strong contrast between dark and bright colours. There is also a large range of tones available in the different colours, allowing striking gradations of tone across the form of the body, and intense modelling of the drapery's folds. The folds can be used to form lines of demarcation between different tones, and also between directions of laying, allowing complex shapes to be filled without ugly, accidental junctions.

In contrast to the three-dimensional modelling of the body, other elements of the design are flatter and more stylized. The face, for instance, is described with a more restricted range of tones, and its wide, almost circular shape gives it a moon-like quality. The eyes are deliberately set far apart to give an expression of calm.

The feathers are also treated in an almost abstract way, using patterns such as 'eyes' and 'bars' found in birds' feathers. These are executed as a flat pattern in a wide range of tones, which balance those used on the figure and create an illusion of form and depth.

METHOD TIPS

Because it is made up of smalti, this project is only suitable as a wall panel. It could be made using either the direct or indirect method (see pages 112 and 114).

• If you are working indirectly you may find that because smalti is so uneven in surface, it does not stick to the paper as firmly as other materials and great care must be taken when turning over the finished piece. A thin layer of adhesive should be applied across the back of the panel before fixing. If the piece is relatively small you may be able to place it on a board

and then position the framed board with its layer of combed adhesive over the pre-glued mosaic, thus sandwiching it safely in position while the whole thing is carefully turned over.

• When the paper is soaked and peeled away, you may find that adhesive shows between the joints. Selecting an adhesive colour that is close in tone to the overall mosaic (in the case of the angel, a dark grey) will mean that in many areas this will not show. Where it is very obvious, for instance in the paler areas of face and hands, the adhesive can be carefully scraped away before it

dries, using a small tool or scalpel. It is recommended that you use a slow-setting product.

• This panel has not been grouted as grouting smalti causes the colour to lose much of its intensity, partly because the direct juxtaposition of the colours is interrupted by grout lines, and partly because the pitted, uneven surface of the glass will inevitably pick up the grout and tone down the colours. If, however, you decide against an ungrouted mosaic, using the indirect method will result in a flatter overall surface which will be easier to grout, and also to clean.

GALLERY

ZOGU

This is a portrait of Zogu (left), an Albanian warlord who was the father of King Zog. It was taken from a 19th-century portrait photograph which was selected as a subject both because of the strength of Zogu's features and the intensity of his expression. His direct gaze emanating out of the picture plane echoes the intense stares of the Byzantine mosaic portraits.

Although taken from an old photograph and inspired by reference to the early Christian era, the technique of execution derives from modern technology. The ancient knowledge on which all mosaics are based – that the eye is able to interpret images made up of many tiny, disparate elements – has been used repeatedly in the age of mechanical reproduction. Newspaper photographs are made up of tiny dots, poster hoardings comprise large patterns of colours and blobs, and new images on computer screens are pixellated, that is, made up of tiny squares. An enlargement of an area of a computer screen looks like the simplest kind of mosaic: a grid of different coloured squares.

To compensate for the highly simplified geometric structure, computer technology applies a more sophisticated technique to colour and tone, called 'dithering'. By making up areas of colour from a wide range of different hues with similar tone, transitions between tones can be blurred and the straight gridded lines disguised. This technique is used here, where a series of colour mixes describe the form of the face. When viewed close up, the mosaic reads as a meaningless jumble, but from a distance the grid disappears and the face emerges clearly.

TWO FIGURES

This small panel (above), (400 x 400mm or 16x16in), is another exercise in the techniques used in The Yellow Table-cloth (see page 92). On this smaller scale the patterns are simplified greatly, but the idea of representing light falling on three-dimensional human forms in an enclosed space is the same.

MAZZINI

The above panel was designed to be fixed in the entrance hall of the building where Guiseppe Mazzini lived during his exile in London. The purpose of the portrait is to convey something of the character of the man who started the campaign for the Unification of Italy and the expression is therefore of crucial importance. Strength of purpose, integrity and devotion to duty are suggested in the austere and commanding face. Mazzini ended his life as an embittered man, disappointed by the establishment of a monarchy rather than a republic, and only returning to Italy disguised as an Englishman. Something of this disillusion can also perhaps be seen in this portrait.

MAKING COPIES OF HISTORICAL
MOSAICS IS AN EXCELLENT
WAY OF LEARNING ABOUT THE
ART. NO AMOUNT OF LOOKING
AT A MOSAIC CAN GIVE YOU
AS MUCH KNOWLEDGE AS
THE SUSTAINED EFFORT AND
OBSERVATION REQUIRED TO
MAKE A COPY. SOME HISTORICAL
EXAMPLES, SUCH AS THE MOSAIC
FROM SAN VITALE IN RAVENNA
ILLUSTRATED, REPRESENT A
DAUNTING CHALLENGE WITH
THEIR IMPOSING FIGURES
AND LAVISH USE OF GOLD,
BUT SMALL DETAILS CAN BE
EXTRACTED AND MADE TO
WORK WELL AS INDIVIDUAL
PANELS. IN THIS CHAPTER WE
WILL EXAMINE HOW TO SELECT
SUITABLE SUBJECTS AND
INTERPRET THEM IN AVAILABLE
MATERIALS TO CREATE COPIES
THAT WORK IN THEIR OWN
RIGHT AS DECORATIVE MOSAICS.

8 HISTORICAL MOSAICS

USING HISTORICAL SOURCES

By copying historical mosaics you will learn techniques of cutting and laying but you will also probably acquire great respect for the craftsmen of the past. At the Mosaic Workshop we have been commissioned to reproduce one of the Roman emblema mosaics from the House of the Tragic Poet at Pompeii. It illustrates a tableaux of seven figures preparing for a theatrical performance and is executed in marble cubes of less than 1mm (0.04in) square. We embarked on the project with the confident assertion that if the Romans could do it, then we could too. It has turned out to be a Herculean task, more difficult than we could ever have imagined. At such a tiny scale the fingers of the human hand are as much use as a bunch of bananas – the pieces have to be manoeuvred with tweezers and needles. In addition, the intensity of observation necessary to differentiate the minute variations in tone in the marble cubes requires total concentration and mental effort. Finally, the rate of progress is enough to try the patience of a saint. The experience has, however, taught us how extremely skilful the Roman craftsmen were, and how much learned knowledge and experience went into the creation of such pieces.

SELECTION

You will learn more from copying an image originally made in mosaic than from translating an image from another art form. Different media obviously have different properties and these exert an influence on the design of a piece. What is easy and natural to execute in one media may be difficult and awkward in another, and this difference will show in the character of the final work. The simple shapes of Matisse's cut-out figure and seaweed collages, for instance, are generated by his instinctive use of the cut paper line, or 'drawing with scissors' as he described it. When these irregular shapes are imitated in mosaic they become a web of conflicting grout lines with tortured angled cuts at the edges, and the spirit of ease and grace in the originals is altogether lost.

It is worthwhile giving careful thought to the selection of a historical mosaic to copy. A general rule is to try to choose something of a scale that will allow you to copy the piece approximately piece for piece. You do not have to use the same size of pieces – you can miniaturize a design by using small pieces – but reinterpreting an image without regard to the number of tesserae will alter the character and feel of the final mosaic. In addition, it is essential to have a photograph of reasonable quality to work from.

SOURCES

Roman floor mosaics, including those uncovered in Roman villas in England, are an excellent design source for geometric patterns. For patterns based on natural forms, such as leaves and vines, the early Christian mosaics at Ravenna provide many examples, as do the Islamic mosaics of the great mosques at Cordoba and Damascus. Images of animals and birds are found in the hunting scenes that were popular across the Roman Empire in the late classical times. Some of the biblical illustrations on Christian churches show a rich selection of God's creation, for instance, the Noah's ark at St Mark's, Venice.

These late medieval illustrative cycles are made up of a series of small narrative scenes, almost like a strip cartoon, and each of the individual frames makes a beautiful and interesting composition in its own right.

Classical mosaics abound with human figures and faces. The most stylized are the black and white linear mosaics found in Ostia, near Rome, dating from the early Imperial Period. The most realistic mosaics were probably produced in the Eastern Roman Empire; these illustrated mythological scenes and introduced the idea of allegorical figures representing geographical phenomena, such as countries and rivers, and later abstract qualities such as luxury and manliness (these were usually accompanied by written labels to aid identification). More everyday subject matter, including farming and fishing scenes, can be found in North African mosaics.

INTERPRETATION

Having selected a mosaic to copy, give careful consideration to the materials to be used. In an ideal world materials should be found to match those used in the original exactly. This will, however, often be impossible. In the case of marble mosaics, for example, there were many stones available in the ancient world whose supplies have now been exhausted. This is even true of mosaics made as recently as fifty years ago, and creates severe difficulties in restoration work. Smalti colours may also be very difficult to match as there is often only a limited range commercially available. Compromises will therefore have to be made, but bear in mind the aim of reproducing the overall quality and character of the original, rather than its every detail. As long as the relationship between your colours and tones follows the original, the overall effect will be similar.

It is also possible to transpose from one material to another without completely losing the sense of likeness and this can have certain advantages. For instance, smalti mosaics can be rendered in vitreous glass, and marble can be represented in unglazed ceramic. These materials are easier to work with and have the added advantage of being much more economical than marble and smalti.

WATER BEAST

This design is based on one of the earliest Roman floor mosaics found in Fishbourne, England, dating from the 1st century. It shows a water beast, half-horse and half-serpent, framed in the ubiquitous guilloche or rope pattern. The original floor is much larger than the small panel shown here, but the clarity and simplicity of the design has made it relatively easy to reduce its scale. It has also been executed in very small pieces

which allows for a further reduction in the size of the finished panel. An important element in the overall character of the piece is the irregularity of outline to which the plain field area is laid, producing an ancient and handmade appearance.

METHOD TIPS

The panel measures 40 x 26cm (16 x 10⅜in) and is made of unglazed ceramic tiles cut down into eighths (that is quartered and then each of the quarters halved). The resulting pieces do not have to be perfectly square as irregularities will add to the liveliness of the effect.

• As it is made of a durable ceramic, this panel can be either set into a floor or fixed to a wall or timber panel.

• The panel can be made using either the direct or indirect method (see pages 112 and 114) but the small sizes of the pieces will make it impossible to stick to a mesh. If you wish to copy a panel piece by piece it is possible either to enlarge a photograph so that the pieces are of the right size or, for extra clarity, to take a careful piece-by-piece tracing and then enlarge this on a photocopier. This copy can then be stuck down securely to a timber board and the tesserae applied directly to the drawing using PVA adhesive (see page 132).

• To begin the mosaic, start with the water beast and then move on to the rope border. You will find that this kind of border has a natural rhythm, and once you have established the most elegant way of laying one section, you can repeat it almost automatically. Finally, you should fill in the plain areas of background.

• Grout the finished piece with grey grout. This will approximate to the colour of the original Roman cement and it will break up dark and light areas equally, giving the piece a harmonious overall effect.

DOVES

This design is taken from the vault of San Vitale in Ravenna and dates from the 6th century. The detail shows a pair of doves against a stylized leaf pattern. The original mosaic is made of smalti. The range of colours can, however, be matched in vitreous glass which, with the black background adding intensity to the colours, looks almost as bright as smalti.

The birds are beautifully observed with their puffed out chests and lively eyes, and it is these details that will be most important in

reproducing the character of the original piece. The strange red line which appears in the tail is clearly not a naturalistic observation and may well represent a repair made at a later date. You can exercise your own judgement about whether to copy such oddities or to correct them.

METHOD TIPS

This panel measures 41.5 x 29.5cm (16¾ x 11¾in) and is made from quarter-cut vitreous glass. It can be made either as a framed panel or stuck directly to a wall. Because of its subject matter it would make an attractive decorative element in a garden or patio.

• Either the direct or indirect method can be used (see pages 112 and 114) or, if the panel is to be hung indoors, you could follow the piece-by-piece method described in the previous project (see page 102).

• If you wish to copy the design piece by piece but want to use it outside, trace the enlarged drawing either reversed on to brown paper for the indirect method or on to a marine plyboard or wall surface for the direct method. Sticking directly to paper, even using EVA, is not recommended as the bond between the board and the paper will not withstand external weather conditions.

• Start the piece by making the birds and then add the leaves and background. The cluster of gold tiles will add sparkle and provide a reference to the more common gold backgrounds of Byzantine and early Christian mosaics.

• When completed, you can grout the panel grey to match the cement of the original, or use a darker grout to help to intensify the colours and produce an overall effect more in keeping with the brilliance of smalti.

THE EMPRESS'S HANDMAIDEN

This portrait head is taken from the church of San Vitale in Ravenna. It is a detail from the panel showing the Empress Theodora with her retinue executed in the 6th century. In the original (see page 98), there is a row of female courtiers whose heads, adorned with jewels, overlap one another as they stand beside the Empress. The head on the far right with the most elaborate headdress was selected for this detail. The background has been simplified to a plain field to enable the image to read more strongly, and the colour of the background has been changed from the original gold to a dark blue. Because of its price, gold is often impractical to use as a background colour, and using a golden colour as a substitute often looks simply like dull brown. The dark blue is used elsewhere in the church of San Vitale as a background colour and it has a depth and richness which is faithfully in character to the original gold mosaic.

As with the doves, this smalti mosaic has been reinterpreted in vitreous glass. The selection of the palette for this design was more difficult as direct equivalents to the flesh tones of the original do not exist. When it comes to rendering flesh tones for this piece, avoid, as always, using too much pink as it can look too sugary and unconvincing.

By making up each area of colour from a mix of two colours, the tones are softened and made more interesting. For example, the pupils of the eyes are made up of a mix of green and brown, rather than the single colour of the original.

METHOD TIPS

The panel is 40cm (16in) square and can be made as a framed panel or stuck directly to a wall (see pages 112 and 114).

• If you wish to copy the design piece by piece but want to use it outside, trace the enlarged drawing either reversed on to brown paper for the indirect method or on to a marine plyboard or wall surface for the direct method. Sticking directly to paper, even using EVA, is not recommended as the bond between the board and the paper will not withstand external weather conditions.

• When making the panel, start with the eyes, nose and mouth and work outwards to the headdress and jewels. Finally, fill in the dark blue background. It is a good idea to run a row of uncut tiles around the edge of the mosaic for a neater effect.

• Grout the finished panel grey. Although this reduces the intensity of the dark blue background, the pale colour helps to unify the flesh tones of the face and creates a closer likeness to the original treatment.

GALLERY

THE ROAD

Although obviously not a copy of a historical mosaic, this piece (above) was inspired by the Roman 'unswept floor' mosaics. The mosaic floors depict items of typical Roman rubbish, such as nut-shells, fishbones and apple cores – sometimes even mice are shown nibbling the debris. This panel was commissioned for a shopping centre and shows an updated version of the idea. The rubbish here is strictly 20th century and consists of sweet wrappers, sandwiches, aluminium cans and cigarette packets.

Because it was intended for use on a floor, the piece was made using the indirect method (see page 114) and rubbish was collected, photocopied, traced and carefully transferred to brown paper.

ROMAN HEAD

Designed for a bathroom wall, this piece (left) is intended to create the illusion of the remains of an ancient mosaic appearing from under a newer finish. The white mosaic crumbles at the edges and the Roman profile is revealed where a large crack has opened up. Although made of vitreous glass, muted colours have been carefully selected to create the impression of natural stone. The laurel wreath and white drapery help to suggest the figure's Roman origin.

VIRGO

This circular marble panel was designed to be set into a garden patio and the subject was inspired by the client's star sign. The commission presented the opportunity to create a figure in the classical style, floating gently against a uniform, cream-coloured background. The problem of defining the pale figure against the pale background was solved by outlining Virgo with a single row of black. Small amounts of black are also used in the surrounding motifs of birds and plants to balance the effect. Lines of laying are important in describing the form of the figure, as in the concentric rings of her breast and the curving contours of her forearms. Tones of white and grey are used to give form to the fold of the figure's drapery.

9 TECHNIQUES, TOOLS & MATERIALS

METHODS

DIRECT METHOD

This method of mosaic allows you to apply tesserae directly on to a panel, so that you can see exactly how the design will look as you are making it. The direct method is not recommended if you require an absolutely flat surface, such as for a floor, as some degree of irregularity in the surface will occur using this method.

Any mosaic material can be fixed directly, but marble and smalti lend themselves well to being used together in this method as they both have a textural quality. The intense colour and reflective properties of smalti complement the subtle crystalline, more muted nature of marble. If the tiles are to be used outside they need to be grouted, as water might penetrate the spaces between them, which could freeze and expand, and the material could then break its bond with the adhesive. An interior panel, however, can be left ungrouted.

MATERIALS, TOOLS & EQUIPMENT

framed MDF board • charcoal • smalti tiles
marble tiles • terracotta tiles • small glue brush
tile nippers • PVA adhesive • stain for frame

STEPS

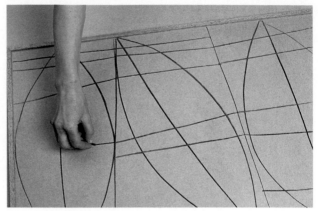

1 Work out a design for your mosaic; it may help to make a sketch indicating colours. It is important when using a highly intense material such as smalti, in combination with something more subtle, to check the way that the colours balance overall. Try to be true to the intensity of the materials when colouring up your design. Do not be tempted to cheat for the sake of an attractive drawing, or you will not learn the lessons this exercise could otherwise reveal. When you are happy with your design, draw the broad outlines on to MDF board using charcoal; this can easily be rubbed out and redrawn if you make a mistake.

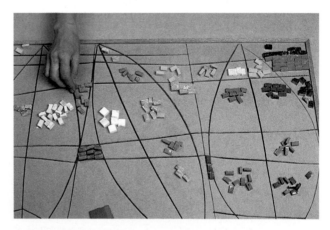

2 Lay the tiles on the board in accordance with your drawing. This enables you to check the balance of colours in relation to one another. If one or two areas seem to dominate the design, this is the moment to change your plans and make a different colour selection.

3 Cut the tesserae to the required size using tile nippers. Unlike thinner materials, to cut marble and smalti, the nippers are placed centrally, rather than at the edge of the tiles. Smalti comes in two forms: in cakes or as small rectangles (above). By cutting a cube of marble in half across the sawn or polished face as here, you can produce riven, rectangular marble tiles to match the thickness and shape of the smalti. Low-fired, crumbly Mexican tiles are easy to cut as the material is soft and easy to fracture.

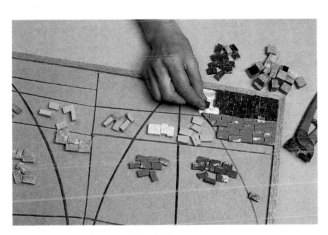

4 Using a paintbrush, spread a small amount of PVA adhesive on a small area of the board, not the tile. Do not spread the glue too thickly, or you may find it squeezes up between the tiles and fouls their surface. Begin to lay the tiles, deciding on the direction in which you wish the lines of coursing to run. Varying the direction will help to give a feeling of liveliness. Where one area of colour meets another, cut the tiles to fit.

5 Build up the design, area by area. Take care how you lay the tiles, particularly smalti and marble which may have uneven surfaces. Ensure you have enough PVA behind each tile, as you need to be certain that it will be held securely in position. Although grout has no real adhesive properties, it can help to key tiles into position. This mosaic will not have this additional safety net, as it will be ungrouted.

6 The flickery smalti contrasts well with the flat, unvarying colour of marble. To keep the outlines of the shapes neat, start by cutting the angle on an edge tile which will be fixed in position where two colours meet. This will help minimize the need for tiny triangles on the edge of an area of colour, which can look messy and unplanned. If a line of colour can only be made to fit by using a number of more irregularly cut tiles, try to lay them towards the centre of an area where they will be better disguised.

INDIRECT METHOD

This method can be used with all mosaic materials that are the same colour on the back and front face. It is particularly recommended where a flat surface is required, for instance on floors and tabletops. The indirect method allows the time-consuming part of the mosaic to be carried out in the workshop or studio so that large-scale jobs can be made off site, in comfort on the workbench. It can be difficult to predict how a piece will look before it is finished, but when the tesserae are stuck to paper it is easy to peel or soak them off again which makes it relatively simple to make changes and adjustments before the work is finally fixed.

The indirect method can be used on curved surfaces if they are curved in one direction only, such as cylindrical columns or barrel vaults because the paper-faced sections are flexible and will easily bend to quite tight radii (20–25cm/8–10in). Surfaces curved in two dimensions, such as domes and spheres, are more challenging and require serious geometry to work out the shape of the flat template.

MATERIALS, TOOLS & EQUIPMENT
brown paper (900gsm) • charcoal or soft pencil
tile nippers • goggles • mosaic tiles
water-soluble glue • cement-based grout
scissors • rubber gloves• grouting squeegee
tiler's sponge • cement-based adhesive
backing surface • small notched trowel
clean, dry rag • mask

STEPS

1 Cut a piece of good quality thick brown kraft paper to the size of the mosaic. Draw out the design on the rough side of the paper with charcoal. Charcoal is a good tool to use as it can be easily corrected with a wipe of the hand.

2 Using tile nippers and wearing goggles, cut the tiles. Build up a pile of each colour tile you need to use, cutting the tiles into quarters. Place the nippers on the edge of the tile, not all the way across or the tile will shatter.

3 Using water-soluble PVA diluted 50:50 with water, stick the pieces face down on the paper (so the grooved side faces up). Apply the glue with a brush to a small area of the paper at a time, enough to stick down about six pieces of tile. Too much glue will saturate the paper and cause it to bubble up. When the glue is dry pick up the paper to test whether the tesserae have held: a crackling noise indicates that they have not.

5 Using a tiler's sponge that has been squeezed almost dry, clean off the back of the mosaic leaving the grout in the joints. Only use a clean face of the sponge and when all the sides are dirty rinse and start again. The pre-grouted mosaic is quite fragile and should not be left in its damp state for more than 20 minutes.

4 When the piece is complete and the glue has dried, the mosaic is ready to be pre-grouted, or grouted from the back. This stops adhesive coming up through the joints and makes it easier to remove the paper facing. Mix up some grout powder with a little water at a time to make a smooth, spreadable paste. Wearing rubber gloves, spread the grout over the mosaic with a squeegee, making sure that all the joints between tiles are filled.

6 Still wearing rubber gloves, mix up some cement-based adhesive with water in a small bowl to make a stiff but workable paste. Make sure that all the powder is absorbed, as loose dry powder at the bottom of the mixture will make the adhesive go off more quickly.

7 Spread the adhesive on the backing surface with a notched trowel. Alternatively, start by spreading on a thin layer and then combing this into ridges. The purpose of the combing is to ensure there is an even layer of adhesive across the surface. Go over areas where the adhesive looks too thin or too lumpy and thick again. Be generous when applying adhesive, particularly if your mosaic has a lot of small pieces.

9 Once the mosaic is in the correct position, wet the paper backing with a sponge, then press the mosaic firmly into the adhesive to ensure that all the separate tesserae are in full contact with the bed. Use your hands or a small flat object such as a grinding stone to press against the face of the mosaic in a circular motion.

8 Lift the mosaic carefully, then turn it over without bending it and place it face down in the adhesive bed. With a small square panel such as this one, hold diagonally opposite corners and position the mosaic in one corner of the frame; the rest can be gently lowered on to the adhesive. At this stage, the whole piece can be pushed around to achieve a perfect fit in the frame, or, in larger mosaics, to ensure a tight fit against the previous section.

10 Keep wetting the paper with a damp sponge until the water-soluble glue has dissolved (about 20 minutes). It is very tempting to try to peel off the paper too soon, but this will only make your life more difficult. If you wait long enough the paper will come away from the face of the tiles easily. Pull the paper gently back across the face of the mosaic, not at right angles to it as this will pull the tiles away from the adhesive. If you are peeling a large area, you can tear the paper into smaller sections as you go. Be careful to keep the discarded brown paper away from the mosaic – as the glue dries out it will stick hard again.

I I The grout will have bled over on to the surface of the tiles and have formed a lumpy surface in the joints. Wash this off while the grout is still wet as it is difficult to correct at a later stage. Using a tiler's sponge, carefully wipe down the face of the mosaic. When all sides of the sponge are dirty, rinse the sponge, squeeze it and start again. Using the sponge when it is dirty will only spread the grout back on again.

I 2 When the adhesive is dry, the mosaic can be grouted again. Pre-grouting will always leave small holes and the edge joint will have to be filled. With larger mosaics the joints between sections will also need filling. To ensure a consistent appearance across the mosaic the whole area should be re-grouted. Wetting the surface can make it easier to apply the grout. Wearing rubber gloves, apply the grout using a squeegee. When dry, remove excess grout with a sponge. The surface can be given a final clean with a damp sponge and clean water. If a dusty residue appears as the surface dries, rub the piece hard with a dry cloth for a final polish.

VARIATIONS OF THE INDIRECT METHOD ARE REFERRED TO IN SPECIFIC PROJECTS. FOR LARGER MOSAICS MADE UP OF SEPARATE SECTIONS, SEE THE FISH TABLE ON PAGE 58. FOR AN EXAMPLE OF THE INDIRECT METHOD USING SMALTI, SEE THE ANGEL ON PAGE 94.

STICKING TO MESH

This method is really a variation of the direct method, where mosaic is stuck directly to a mesh before being stuck to the backing surface. It can be used with all mosaic materials but works best where the size of the individual pieces is not so small as to lie unevenly on the mesh. It is a good method to use where the back and front faces of the material are very different, as with glazed tiles. The main advantage it has over the direct method is that, as with the indirect method, the work of assembling the mosaic can be done sitting at a table in the workshop or studio and then transferred to the final location in one piece, or in manageable sections. A more advanced application of the method is for jobs that require epoxy grout. It is not possible to pre-grout with epoxy grout and so the indirect method is not easy. If the piece has to be made in the workshop, fixing to mesh is an option worth considering. Because the tiles are stuck with PVA, it is not a technique that is recommended for wet areas or for outdoors.

MATERIALS, TOOLS & EQUIPMENT

paper • charcoal or marker pen • clingfilm
masking tape • mosaic or ceramic tiles
tile nippers • goggles • mesh • small brush
non-water-soluble PVA • scissors
cement-based adhesive • rubber gloves
backing surface • small notched trowel
cement-based grout • grouting squeegee
clean, dry rag

STEPS

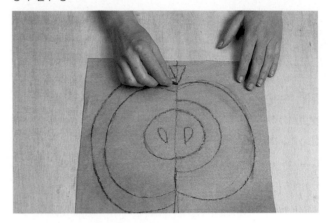

1 Cut a piece of thick craft paper to the size of the mosaic panel and draw on your design in a strong line, for instance a marker pen or dark charcoal. It will be easier to make graceful curves if you draw quickly and with confidence.

2 Cut out a piece of clingfilm larger than the craft paper and stick this down over the paper and secure to the work surface with strips of masking tape. This will prevent the mosaic sticking to the paper.

3 Cut glazed ceramic tiles into narrow strips with a tile cutter. To do this, first score a line into the face of the tile by pressing down with the scoring wheel. Enough pressure is required to produce a visible line. Then place the tile in the cutter so that the snapper is on each side of the score line. Squeeze the handles to make the tile break along the line.

5 Cut out a piece of mesh slightly larger than the mosaic panel and tape this over the drawing. Begin to stick down the tile pieces, shaping them further as necessary with the nippers. Brush non-water-soluble glue over the mesh in small areas at a time. Do not worry about it sticking to the clingfilm as it will peel off easily when the glue is dry.

4 Then cut the narrow strips of tile down further with tile nippers. As with glass tiles, place the nippers on the edge of the tile at the angle of the cut required. Always wear goggles when cutting tiles as sharp fragments of tile can fly everywhere.

6 When the mosaic piece is finished and the adhesive is dry, remove the masking tape and clingfilm and carefully trim off the excess mesh around the mosaic with scissors.

7 To stick the mesh-backed mosaic to the backing surface use a suitable cement-based adhesive. Mix the adhesive with water to make a thick, spreadable paste and apply it to the backing surface with a 3mm (⅛in) notched trowel. This will create an even, adhesive bed thin enough not to come up between the joints and thick enough to hold the tiles. Place the mesh-backed mosaic on the adhesive and press down firmly. Even on vertical surfaces, the adhesive should hold the panel in position immediately.

8 When the adhesive is dry, mix up some grout powder with a little water to make a smooth, spreadable paste. The powder is very fine and the water should be added gradually so as not to make the mixture sloppy.

9 Apply the grout over the mosaic with a grouting squeegee. Work the grout into the joints between the tiles.

10 Because this piece was made with porous glazed tiles the grout dries very quickly and the excess grout forms a loose powder that can easily be brushed off. Finish the mosaic by polishing it with a clean, dry cloth. Further wetting at this stage would only cause the grout to smear.

CASTING

This method is a useful technique when you want to use items with a variety of thicknesses, but at the same time to create a finished surface that is flat enough to work on. A slab created using this method is strong but heavy, and would be just as suitable for use outside in the garden as in the house.

MATERIALS, TOOLS & EQUIPMENT

paper • casting frame • charcoal
marble tiles • water-soluble PVA • tile nippers
rubber gloves • flat bed trowel
grouting squeegee • sponge • petroleum jelly
cloth • sharp washed sand • Portland cement
metal lath or chicken wire • plastic sheeting
screwdriver • wooden board

STEPS

1 Cut a piece of craft paper fractionally smaller all round than the casting frame you plan to use. Draw the design outlines on the paper in charcoal; this design is made up of a series of simple concentric circles.

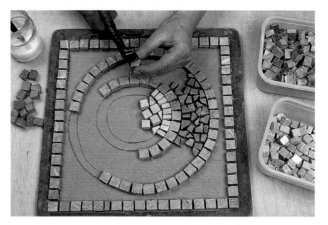

2 Stick marble cubes on to the paper with water-soluble PVA glue diluted 1:1 with water, leaving small spaces between each cube. Build up the design area by area, cutting the tiles with tile nippers where necessary to fit the drawn design. When complete, set aside to dry. Although this mosaic is made from marble cubes, the technique shown works with a wide range of mosaic materials.

3 When the mosaic is dry, mix the grout. Half-fill a small plastic container with water, then add cement until it achieves a thick, creamy consistency. Wearing rubber gloves to prevent contact with the grout, which is very drying to the skin, trowel the grout on to the mosaic, pushing it into all the joints with a grout squeegee. Soak a sponge in water and squeeze it out thoroughly, then use it to clean away the excess grout.

5 To make the body of the paving slab, mix three parts sand to one part cement in a bucket, then add water until the mixture is workable; it is better to add too much water than too little. Trowel the mix on to the grouted mosaic.

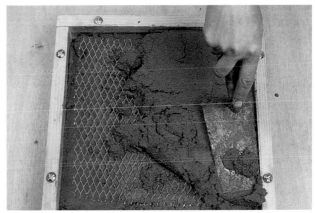

4 Using a cloth, spread a layer of petroleum jelly over the inside of the casting frame, making sure it is applied right into the corners. This will work as a release agent. Place the grouted mosaic into the frame, paper side down.

6 When the sand and cement mixture is halfway up the inside of the frame, cover it with expanded metal lath or chicken wire to reinforce it. Fill the frame to the top with the remaining sand and cement mixture. Tamp it flat with the back of the trowel and cover the frame with plastic sheeting. Leave to dry for a week.

7 Unscrew the casting frame one batten at a time. The mosaic slab can now be removed. Place a board on top of the slab, sandwich it between your hands, and turn it over.

9 Peel away the paper carefully from one corner of the slab. Pull flat to the slab rather than at a 90-degree angle, which would put stress on the mosaic tiles. Once the paper has been removed, regrout the slab from the front (see step 3).

8 The craft paper will now be facing upwards. Rub a wet sponge over the paper repeatedly until it turns a dark brown colour. The paper is now ready to peel off.

10 Wearing rubber gloves, sponge the excess grout off the face of the mosaic. Rewrap the slab in plastic sheeting and leave it for another week. The completed mosaic can then be laid in the garden. The completed mosaic will be weatherproof but may need cleaning occasionally with a suitable cleaner.

FIXING MOSAICS TO 3-D OBJECTS

Mosaic can be fixed to all sorts of three-dimensional objects such as flower pots, bottles and vases. Bear in mind that exposed edges, such as at the rims, will be vulnerable to knocking, and that the surfaces will inevitably be uneven. When sticking directly to vertical or curved surfaces it is important to use a glue that will hold the pieces in position straightaway, such as a cement-based adhesive or silicone.

MATERIALS, TOOLS & EQUIPMENT

charcoal or marker pen • mosaic or ceramic tiles • hammer • cement-based adhesive small tool or palette knife • cement-based grout rubber gloves • dry, clean cloth

STEPS

1 Plan how you are going to decorate the pot. Draw guidelines on the surface with charcoal or marker pen. Using different colours and patterns in bands or discreet areas will probably be more interesting than a totally random mosaic effect.

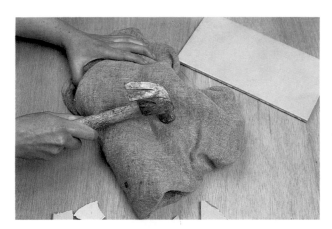

2 This pot will be decorated with broken glazed ceramic tiles. To break tiles, it is a good idea to wrap them up in an old cloth to prevent fragments flying everywhere. Gently smash the tiles with a hammer.

3 Mix up a small quantity of a suitable slow-setting cement-based adhesive. Don't mix up too much since it will go off and be wasted. A slow-setting adhesive will give you time to work. Apply a small area of adhesive on the pot (enough to stick on two or three pieces of tile) using a small tool or palette knife, and stick pieces of tile in place following the guidelines. Gradually work your way around the pot. Do not lean the pot over on to areas that you have decorated unless the adhesive is dry and the pieces are firmly fixed.

4 When you have finished sticking and the adhesive is dry, you can grout the piece. Mix the grout powder with water to make a thick paste, adding the water gradually so as not to make it too sloppy. Wearing rubber gloves, spread the grout all over the surface and into the joints. On a three-dimensional object it is easier to grout with your hands than with a squeegee.

5 With porous tiles the grout will dry very quickly. Rub off the excess grout with your hands. If you have used terracotta tiles you may not want to see any of the edges exposed at the joints so you will need to keep the joints as full of grout as possible. To finish the piece, give it a final polish with a dry, clean cloth.

TOOLS

TILE NIPPERS

Tile nippers are the most versatile and essential tool for making mosaic. The sharp teeth are tungsten-tipped and can be used to cut all mosaic materials. Both the front and the back of the nippers can be used for cutting, and they can be used with or without the spring. Blunt nippers are sometimes better for cutting marble, and all nippers acquire a distinct character in time. Most materials cut best if the nippers are placed only at the edge of the tile rather than half-way across. The angle at which the nippers are held will dictate the angle of the cut.

TILE CUTTERS

This tool combines a scoring wheel and a snapper. The wheel is run along the line of the cut and then the tile is placed in the snapper so that pressure is applied on either side of the score line. Tile cutters are useful for cutting larger tiles (over 2.5cm/1in square) and for neat geometric cuts such as triangles. Larger cutters are available for thicker and harder tiles; they work on the same principle but the wheel and snapper are fixed to a long handle which runs along a track above a fixed bed on which the tile is located. The long handle gives greater leverage when snapping the tiles.

GLASS CUTTER

This is a tool for scoring glass along the line of a cut. It can have a fixed, hard point or a cutting wheel which sometimes has an oil reservoir to lubricate the wheel and ensure continuous contact with the surface of the glass. After scoring, the glass can be snapped holding each side of the line firmly with thumb and fingers or by placing pliers close to one side of the line and then snapping. For small pieces of glass it is easier to use the snapper on a tile cutter. Glass cutters are necessary for cutting stained glass and can also be used to score gold and silver tiles for a neater cut.

GROUTING SQUEEGEE

This tool has a wooden handle and a rubber blade and is used to work grout into the joints between the tesserae. It can be used for pre-grouting and for grouting from the front on vertical and horizontal surfaces. It is effective for small- and medium-sized pieces but over large areas the wrist movement required can become tiring. A flat-bed squeegee is useful for applying grout over larger areas.

SMALL-NOTCHED TROWEL

A trowel with a notch of 3mm (⅛in) is recommended for fixing mosaics. The trowel is used to apply cement-based adhesive to the backing surface, both vertical and horizontal. Combing the adhesive bed will ensure a thin, even layer across the surface.

When fixing a mosaic outdoors, it is important that the ridges do not remain as they will form cavities which could fill with water, and this could freeze and push off the tiles. If the mosaic is very firmly pressed into the adhesive the ridges should flatten out, but it is better to use a thick-bed trowel that has extra long teeth at each end, allowing a solid bed of constant thickness.

SMALL TROWEL

A plastering tool, this little trowel is invaluable for applying cement-based adhe-sive to small, awkward areas. It is also used in the direct method to apply small areas of adhesive to the backing surface.

TWEEZERS

These can be useful when working on micro-mosaics, that is, mosaics made up of very small pieces. They can be used to pick up pieces and manoeuvre them into position in conjunction with a small pointed tool such as a dental probe or darning needle.

MASK

It is advisable to wear a protective face mask when cutting mosaic materials as this will create fine dust which should not be inhaled. It is particularly important to wear a mask if you are doing a lot of cutting at once, for instance preparing a stock of quartered glass tiles or riven marble pieces.

GOGGLES

Small slivers of material can fly upwards when cutting and eyes should be protected by spectacles or goggles.

TILER'S SPONGE

These sponges have a fine, dense structure and are designed to be very absorbent, both of water and of fine powders such as grout. It is much quicker to clean a mosaic with a special tiler's sponge than an ordinary household sponge, and it will not leave smears or a dusty residue.

HAMMER AND HARDIE

These are the traditional mosaicist's cutting tools. A tungsten-tipped hammer is brought down on marble or smalti tesserae resting on a sharp chisel or hardie embedded in a tree trunk or other solid base.

MATERIALS

There are several different types of tile, or tesserae, that can be used in mosaic. The most readily available and easy to use are listed below.

GLAZED CERAMIC

A glazed ceramic is a tile where the colour has been applied to the surface as a thin layer in the form of a glaze. These tiles therefore have a markedly different front and back face. Because of this, it is virtually impossible to use them in the indirect method. They come in many sizes, patterns, thicknesses and qualities. Some are fired at a very high temperature and will resist frost and moisture penetration, but many are porous and would crack and crumble if used outdoors. When selecting tiles to use in a mosaic, it is better to choose ones of a similar thickness, as this makes the process simpler, and the finished result looks more attractive. Glazed ceramic tiles can be smashed with a hammer, cut more neatly in straight lines with a tile cutter or nibbled into shape with tile nippers.

UNGLAZED CERAMIC

These are manufactured mosaic tiles 2cm (¾in) or 2.5cm (1in) square and approximately 4mm (0.15in) thick. They are uniformly coloured throughout and are identical on the front and back face. They have crisp, square edges making them suitable for cut-piece work. They are available in a limited range of muted, earthy colours, including some that are speckled or patterned with tiny dots of different shades. They are easy to cut with tile nippers although the paler colours may be more likely to shatter. Accurate geometric cuts such as triangles are easier to achieve using a tile cutter and after scoring the line.

VITREOUS GLASS

These tiles are manufactured from opaque glass and are usually 2cm (¾in) square and 4mm (0.15in) thick. They are supplied 'paper-faced' in sheets that are approximately 35cm (14in) square. Vitreous glass tiles are uniformly coloured throughout but the back face is textured to provide a better key for the adhesive. They are available in a wide range of colours, particularly in the green range and, to a lesser extent, in blues and greys. The colours are limited by the manufacturing process and there are no strong pinks or purples. Some of the tiles are shot through with gold veins. They can be cut easily with tile nippers but can produce sharp splinters of glass that should always be cleared up with a brush rather than your hands.

SMALTI

This is the term for Venetian enamelled glass. The colours available in this material are very intense and cover a wide tonal range in each hue. They are cut from 'omelettes' of glass into rectangles measuring approximately 1.5 x 1cm (⅝ x ½in). Both front and back faces tend to be uneven and irregular and this glass is not, therefore, used for floors or other flat surfaces. Smalti is handmade, probably in the same way as in Roman times, and is, as a result, relatively expensive. It can either be cut with a hammer and hardie in the traditional way, or with tile nippers.

MARBLE

Marble cubes can be cut to any size. They are usually cut on a wet saw from marble tiles and therefore have a polished face. The back face will be unpolished but may bear the diagonal marks of a saw-blade. Tiles are usually 7mm (0.3in) or 1cm (½in) thick, which is an easy thickness to cut with nippers. Traditionally, marble is cut with a hammer and hardie; with thicker marble this is the best way to shape the pieces. When laid on floors, marble can be polished, after first ensuring that the surface is perfectly flat. Marble is polished using a large and messy machine and is therefore only practical for relatively large areas. When marble is cut either with a hammer or nippers, the exposed face has an uneven, crystalline surface which can be used on wall mosaics and panels; this is called 'riven' marble. Marble can be used both inside and outside. In wet areas, such as showers, some marbles are very porous and

might become stained; it is advisable to use proprietary sealants in such conditions.

GOLD & SILVER

These tiles are made from sheets of glass covered with gold or silver leaf, which is itself covered with a very thin layer of transparent glass to protect the metallic surface. They are usually 2cm (¾in) square and 4mm (0.15in) thick. Gold tiles are commonly backed with dark green glass, while silver ones have a blue back; these reverse faces can also be used. The metal leaf seen through the transparent glass gives these tiles a beautiful glistening quality. 'Ripple' gold tiles are also available, with an uneven, bubbly surface. In Italy it is possible to find a wide range of different metallic colours, ranging from pale golds to copper and bronze. Because they are made with real gold and silver leaf, these tiles are expensive and only used in large areas as a conscious display of extravagance.

A D H E S I V E S
& G R O U T S

All glues and grouts have different properties. Use this guide and the accompanying table to decide which adhesives to use for your particular mosaic requirements.

C E M E N T - B A S E D
A D H E S I V E

This is tiling adhesive that has developed from traditional sand and cement and has been designed to give better adhesion and easier working characteristics. It is available with different properties:

Rapid setting For situations where you need to finish grouting quickly.

Exterior This adhesive is frost-resistant and waterproof.

Flexible With a latex additive this adhesive has a greater tolerance of movement and is designed for use on timber backings.

These different types of cement-based adhesive are all proprietary products and the manufacturers' recommendations will vary according to which brand you use. Always study the instructions carefully and if you are in doubt, most companies have technical advice departments you can contact. In general, it is better to use powder-based products which you mix up yourself to your own desired quantity and consistency rather than ready-mixed tubs which can dry out too quickly.

PVA

Polyvinyl acetate (PVA) is a white liquid glue that comes in two basic forms:

Water-soluble This type sticks firmly but will dissolve when exposed to water. It is used in the indirect method to stick to brown paper. Other water-soluble glues, such as wallpaper paste or gum arabic, can be used for this purpose but they do not stick as firmly. Water-soluble PVA is sometimes known as school glue and usually needs to be diluted 50:50 with water.

Non-water-soluble As its name suggests, this type of PVA forms an irreversible bond and is used for the direct method of mosaic. Waterproof wood glues and good quality PVA bought from hardware stores are usually in this category. They should be used undiluted and applied to the backing surface with a small brush which must be cleaned carefully after use.

Make sure that you are using the right type of PVA for the job. If you are in any doubt, do a test by sticking a piece of mosaic to paper, letting the glue dry and then wetting the paper for 20 minutes. If the mosaic comes off the paper the glue is water-soluble, if not the bond is irreversible.

E V A

Ethylene vinyl acetate (EVA) is a kind of irreversible, non-water-soluble PVA that is suitable for use outdoors. It can be used for the direct method of mosaic, sticking materials to marine ply or exterior-grade boards.

S I L I C O N E

Available from hardware stores, silicone is generally sold in cartridges for use in a mastic gun. It comes as a thick, clear jelly and can be used for sticking glass to glass or any other surface. It dries thick but still slightly rubbery, thus allowing the expansion and contraction that is characteristic of glass. It is water-resistant so surfaces to be stuck must be dry, while surfaces to be kept clean, such as your fingers, can be dampened. Care must be taken not to get the silicone on the face of the glass as it will be impossible to remove. Ordinary silicone is slightly cloudy but this is not usually noticeable in a thin adhesive layer. If absolute transparency is required, perfectly clear silicone is available from specialist glaziers.

SAND & CEMENT

Sand and cement mixed in the proportion of 3:1 or 4:1, and in a bed of a minimum depth of 2.5cm (1in), can be used to fix floor mosaics. It is the best medium to use if you are using cubes of different thicknesses, or a mixture of materials of different thicknesses, as they can be beaten into the screed to create a flat surface. This can be done with both the direct and indirect method. It is a difficult job to achieve a level surface and requires a lot of experience. Sand and cement are also used to cast mosaic paving slabs reinforced with stainless steel mesh. The sand should be sharp washed sand and the cement can be grey or white Portland cement.

CEMENT-BASED GROUT

Grout contains far less cement than cement-based adhesives and is consequently far less sticky. Its purpose is to fill the gaps between the pieces with a weak mix that will allow some movement in the piece without causing cracking. Proprietary grouts are available in powder form to mix with water and in a range of colours including grey, black, ivory and white. Colourants are also available to make coloured grouts, and acrylic or emulsion paints can also be used as coloured mixes. These should only be used on relatively small pieces where the whole area can be grouted in one batch as it will be very difficult to mix a second batch to match exactly. Some manufacturers produce mixes that improve the water resistance and flexibility of the grout. Ready-mixed grouts are also available but these tend to be harder to apply and clean off the mosaic. Most difficult of all to use are the products that are sold as both grout and adhesive: for mosaic work they are not sticky enough to hold the small pieces securely, and yet they are too sticky to clean off the surface without ripping up the mosaic. Manufacturers often recommend fine grout for the narrow joints in mosaic work but in practice the coarser grouts designed for wider joints seem to work just as well and are considerably easier to clean off the surface.

EPOXY GROUT

This is a two-part, resin-based grout which forms a joint that is both waterproof and flexible. It is specified in areas where hygiene is of great importance and where tiling is required to form a waterproof barrier.

BACKINGS

The following list is a guide to the backings that are suitable for mosaic work. Check that you use the correct backing for the type of mosaic you are making.

PLASTER & PLASTERBOARD

This is not a suitable backing in wet areas such as showers, but in dry areas if primed with a dilute solution of PVA it forms a good base for cement-based adhesives. If the plaster is painted, the adhesive will stick to the paint but the bond to the wall will only be as good as the bond of the paint to the plaster. Therefore, if the paint is flaking and comes off easily it should be removed.

SAND & CEMENT SCREEDS & RENDERS

Because the adhesives are cement based, these sand and cement backings are the perfect surfaces to fix to. No primer is required but the surface should be as even as possible to avoid irregularities in that of the mosaic.

TIMBER FLOORS

Before tiling, floorboards should always be boarded over with plywood at least 1cm (½in) thick. The plywood should be screwed down at 22.5cm (9in) intervals and in wet areas such as bathrooms, exterior-grade or marine ply should be used. Joints between boards will always tend to suffer from movement and should be avoided if possible or positioned with care, for instance to coincide with a straight joint in the mosaic.

TIMBER PANELS & TABLETOPS

For interior use, medium density fibreboard (MDF) is a good backing material because it is very stable. When fixing mosaic to boards, the backing should be stiff enough not to bend and crack off the tiles. The thickness of board required will depend on the size of the panel, but 12mm (½in) is probably sufficient for those up to 90cm (36in) square. For larger panels, the overall weight should be taken into consideration and it might be better to brace the back with battens rather than to use a thick and heavy board.

For outside use, panels should be made of marine or exterior-grade plywood. The edges of a mosaic panel will always be vulnerable unless enclosed by some kind of frame. A mosaic edging stuck to the sides of the board will be even more vulnerable, both to accidental knocks and to the expansion and contraction of the timber. A better solution is a simple timber frame made from a batten glued and pinned to the edge of the board. For outside use the frame should be made of hardwood; aluminium angle can also be used, as can flexible brass or copper strips.

TILE-BACKER BOARD

This is a mineral fibre board designed to form a rigid and stable backing for tiling in wet areas such as showers. It also forms an ideal surface for mosaic.

TERRACOTTA

Flower pots and planters can be covered in mosaic using cement-based adhesive. The terracotta is very porous and should first be primed with a dilute solution of PVA.

GLASS

Both sheets of glass and glass objects can be covered in mosaic using clear silicone adhesive. They are most effective with light shining through them – when hung in windows or made as candle holders. Black grout will create a stained glass effect.

OTHER SURFACES

Most surfaces that are stiff and rigid are suitable for covering in mosaic. If they have a hard, impervious finish, such as metal or plastic laminate, they should be primed with a proprietary primer before an application of cement-based adhesive.

TEMPLATES

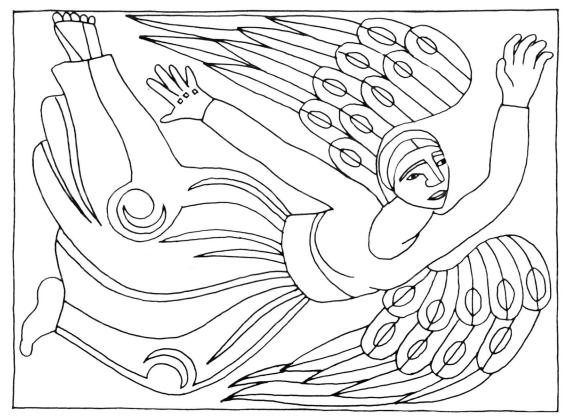

page 94

page 104

page 54

page 55

page 55

page 54

page 90

page 28

page 15

page 14

page 15

page 14

page 66

page 106

page 80

page 58

page 44

page 102

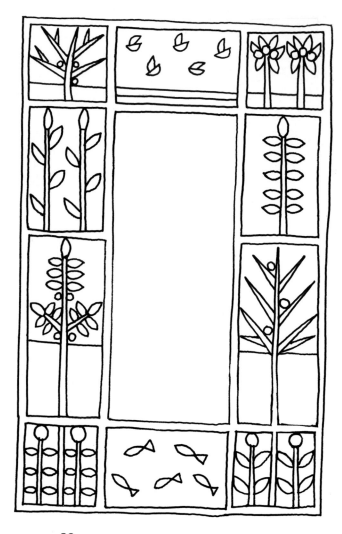

page 32

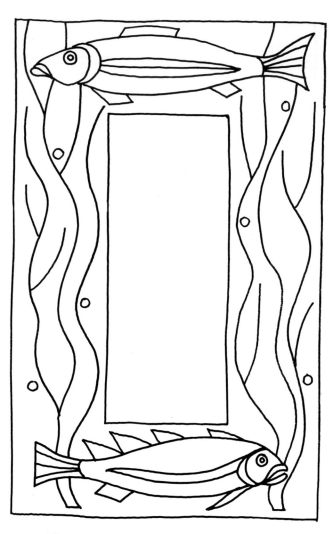

page 68

page 57

page 18

page 92

page 42

ADHESIVES AND BACKINGS

	INDOOR							
	WALLS			FLOORS				PANELS AND TABLETOPS
	WET AREAS		DRY AREAS	WET AREAS		DRY AREAS		
	EXISTING CERAMIC TILES	TILE BACKER BOARD/SAND/CEMENT RENDER	PLASTER/PLASTER BOARD	SAND/CEMENT SCREED	MARINE OR EXTERIOR PLY	SAND/CEMENT SCREED	PLYWOOD	TIMBER OR MDF
DIRECT METHOD	CEMENT-BASED ADHESIVE ON PROPRIETARY PRIMER FOR IMPERVIOUS SURFACES	CEMENT-BASED ADHESIVE	CEMENT-BASED ADHESIVE ON DILUTE (50:50) PVA PRIMER	CEMENT-BASED ADHESIVE	CEMENT-BASED ADHESIVE WITH FLEXIBLE AD-MIX * SEE FOOTNOTE	CEMENT-BASED ADHESIVE	CEMENT-BASED ADHESIVE WITH FLEXIBLE AD-MIX * SEE FOOTNOTE	NON WATER-SOLUBLE PVA OR CEMENT-BASED ADHSIVE WITH FLEXIBLE ADDITIVE * SEE FOOTNOTE
INDIRECT METHOD	AS ABOVE	AS ABOVE	AS ABOVE	CEMENT-BASED ADHESIVE OR SAND/CEMENT (3:1 OR 4:1)	AS ABOVE	CEMENT-BASED ADHESIVE OR SAND/CEMENT (3:1 OR 4:1)	AS ABOVE	AS ABOVE
MESH METHOD	NOT RECOMMENDED	NOT RECOMMENDED	CEMENT-BASED ADHESIVE ON DILUTE (50:50) PRIMER	NOT RECOMMENDED	NOT RECOMMENDED	CEMENT-BASED ADHESIVE	AS ABOVE	AS ABOVE

	OUTDOOR					UNDERWATER FOUNTAINS AND POOLS
	WALLS	FLOORS	PANELS AND TABLETOPS	OTHER		
	SAND/CEMENT RENDER	SAND/CEMENT SCREED	MARINE OR EXTERIOR GRADE PLY WITH HARDWOOD FRAME	TERRACOTTA POTS	CAST SLABS	SAND/CEMENT SCREED
DIRECT METHOD	FROST-PROOF CEMENT-BASED ADHESIVE	FROST-PROOF CEMENT-BASED ADHESIVE	EVA OR FROST-PROOF CEMENT-BASED ADHESIVE WITH FLEXIBLE ADMIX * SEE FOOTNOTE	FROST-PROOF CEMENT-BASED ADHESIVE ON DILUTE PVA PRIMER	SAND/CEMENT (3:1 OR 4:1) ON STAINLESS STEEL MESH	FROST-PROOF CEMENT-BASED ADHESIVE
INDIRECT METHOD	FROST-PROOF CEMENT-BASED ADHESIVE	FROST-PROOF CEMENT-BASED ADHESIVE OR SAND/CEMENT (3:1 OR 4:1)	FROST-PROOF CEMENT-BASED ADHESIVE WITH FLEXIBLE ADMIX * SEE FOOTNOTE	NOT RECOMMENDED	AS ABOVE	AS ABOVE
MESH METHOD	NOT RECOMMENDED	NOT RECOMMENDED	NOT RECOMMENDED	NOT RECOMMENDED	NOT RECOMMENDED	NOT RECOMMENDED

* FOOTNOTE: SOME PROPRIETARY ADHESIVES CONTAIN AN INTEGRAL FLEXIBLE INGREDIENT FOR USE ON TIMBER BACKING

GLASS

TO MOSAIC GLASS OBJECTS, USE THE DIRECT METHOD WITH A TRANSPARENT SILICONE ADHESIVE.

GROUT

GROUT IS ESSENTIAL FOR ALL INDOOR AND OUTDOOR MOSAICS WITH THE EXCEPTION OF PIECES MADE ON PLASTER/PLASTERBOARD OR TIMBER OR MDF PANELS AND TABLETOPS — IN SUCH CASES IT IS OPTIONAL. EPOXY GROUT IS RECOMMENDED FOR USE ON UNDERWATER MOSAICS.

MOSAIC MATERIALS

	INDOOR				
	WALLS		FLOORS	TIMBER-BACKED WALL PANELS	TABLETOPS
	WET AREAS	DRY AREAS	WET/DRY AREAS		
DIRECT METHOD	GLAZED/UNGLAZED CERAMIC; POLISHED MARBLE (SURFACE MAY NEED SEALING)	GLAZED/UNGLAZED CERAMIC; VITREOUS GLASS; SMALTI; POLISHED AND HONED MARBLE; RIVEN MARBLE	UNGLAZED CERAMIC; VITREOUS GLASS (AREAS OF LIGHT TRAFFIC ONLY); POLISHED AND HONED MARBLE (SURFACE MAY NEED SEALING)	GLAZED/UNGLAZED CERAMIC; VITREOUS GLASS; SMALTI; POLISHED AND HONED MARBLE; RIVEN MARBLE; PEBBLES	GLAZED/UNGLAZED CERAMIC; VITROUS GLASS; POLISHED AND HONED MARBLE;
INDIRECT METHOD	UNGLAZED CERAMIC; VITREOUS GLASS; POLISHED MARBLE (SURFACE MAY NEED SEALING)	UNGLAZED CERAMIC; VITREOUS GLASS; SMALTI; POLISHED AND HONED MARBLE; RIVEN MARBLE	AS ABOVE	UNGLAZED CERAMIC; VITREOUS GLASS; SMALTI; POLISHED AND HONED MARBLE; RIVEN MARBLE	UNGLAZED CERAMIC; VITROUS GLASS; POLISHED AND HONED MARBLE
MESH METHOD	NOT RECOMMENDED	GLAZED/UNGLAZED CERAMIC; VITREOUS GLASS; SMALTI; POLISHED AND HONED MARBLE; RIVEN MARBLE	AS ABOVE FOR DRY AREAS; MESH METHOD NOT RECOMMENDED FOR WET AREAS	GLAZED/UNGLAZED CERAMIC; VITREOUS GLASS; SMALTI; POLISHED AND HONED MARBLE; RIVEN MARBLE	GLAZED/UNGLAZED CERAMIC; VITREOUS GLASS; POLISHED AND HONED MARBLE

	OUTDOOR				UNDERWATER FOUNTAINS AND POOLS
	WALLS	FLOORS	PANELS	TABLETOPS	
			MARINE PLY BACKING	MARINE PLY OR CONCRETE	
DIRECT METHOD	FROST-PROOF CERAMIC TILES; VITREOUS GLASS; UNGLAZED CERAMIC; POLISHED AND HONED MARBLE; RIVEN MARBLE; PEBBLES	UNGLAZED CERAMIC; POLISHED AND HONED MARBLE; PEBBLES	FROST-PROOF GLAZED CERAMIC; VITREOUS GLASS; UNGLAZED CERAMIC; SMALTI; POLISHED AND HONED MARBLE; RIVEN MARBLE; PEBBLES	FROST-PROOF CERAMIC TILES; VITREOUS GLASS; UNGLAZED CERAMIC; POLISHED AND HONED MARBLE	FROST-PROOF GLAZED CERAMIC TILES; VITREOUS GLASS; UNGLAZED CERAMIC
INDIRECT METHOD	UNGLAZED CERAMIC; VITREOUS GLASS; SMALTI; POLISHED AND HONED MARBLE	UNGLAZED CERAMIC; POLISHED AND HONED MARBLE	VITREOUS GLASS; UNGLAZED CERAMIC; SMALTI; POLISHED AND HONED MARBLE; RIVEN MARBLE	VITREOUS GLASS; UNGLAZED CERAMIC; POLISHED AND HONED MARBLE	VITREOUS GLASS; UNGLAZED CERAMIC
MESH METHOD	NOT RECOMMENDED	NOT RECOMMENDED	NOT RECOMMENDED	NOT RECOMMENDED	NOT RECOMMENDED

SUPPLIERS

Edgar Udny & Co. Ltd
314 Balham High Road
London SW17 7AA
Tel: 0171 767 8181
Ceramic, glass and
smalti.Fixing materials.
Mail order service available.

Reed Harris
27 Carnwath Road
London SW6 3HR
Tel: 0171 736 7511
Ceramic, glass and marble.
Fixing materials. Mail
order service available.

Lead & Light Warehouse
35a Hartland Road
London NW1 8BD
Tel: 0171 485 0997
Stained glass. They will not
cut the glass
for you, but sell glass-
cutting materials. Mail
order services available.

Mosaic Workshop
Unit B
443-449 Holloway Road
London N7 6LJ
Tel: 0171 263 2997

Mosaic Workshop Shop
1a Princeton Street
London W1R 4AX
Tel: 0171 404 9249
Glass, smalti, ceramic and
marble. Adhesives, tools,
boards and all associated
paraphernalia are available
from the Workshop and
the Shop. The Workshop
also runs courses. Mail
order services available.

Tower Ceramics Ltd.
91 Parkway
Camden Town
London NW1 9PP
Tel: 0171 485 7192
Ceramic tiles, marble and
terracotta. Adhesives,
grout, cleaning materials
for marble and terracotta,
and all associated tools.

Paul Fricker Ltd
Well Park
Willeys Avenue
Exeter
Devon EX2 8BE
Tel: 01392 2786367

INDEX

Entries in italics refer to
projects

Adhesives, 132, 133
Andamenti, 49
Angel, 94, 95
Angles, 51
Animal panels, 53-57
Anteater, 54
Armadillo, 55
Astronaut, 90, 91

Backgrounds, 52
Backings, 134, 135
Bathroom panels, 11,
23, 34
Bird tile, 28
Borders, 82, 83

Casting, 122-125
Ceramic mirror, 32, 33
Ceramic table, 80, 81
Circles, 52
Colour
changing, 12
faces and figures, of, 88
grout, of, 26, 27
hue, 24
intensity, 24
planning, 26
tonal range, 13
tonal transition, 93
tone, 24
ungrouted mosaic, 26
use of, 23
Cones, 73
Contrast
aspects of, 37
cutting, creation by,
38, 39
Crockery tabletop, 16, 17

Design
components, 12
principles of, 9
vocabulary of, 12
Diamonds, 46
Direct method, 112, 113
Doves, 104, 105

Empress's handmaiden,
106, 107

Faces and figures
angel, 94, 95
astronaut, 90, 91
colour, 88
laying, 89
mosaic, in, 87-97
movement, 88
proportion, 88
tone, 88
Fan, 52
Fish men, 35
Fish mosaic, 42, 43
Fish table, 58, 59
Food panels, 21
Fruit and vegetables,
14, 15

Garden pavement, 37
Glass, 135
Glass cutter, 128
Glazed ceramic, 130
tabletop, 30, 31
Glazed tile tabletop, 40,
41
Goggles, using, 129
Gold and silver panel,
70, 71
Gold tiles, 131
Groucho Club, entrance
to, 46
Grout
cement-based, 133
colour, 26, 27
epoxy, 133
lines, effect of, 49
Grouting squeegee,
129

Hammer and hardie, 129
Historical mosaics,
99-109
image, copying, 100
interpretation, 101
Historical sources,
using, 100, 101
House of the Tragic

Poet, Pompeii, 100
Human figure
composition, 88, 89

Indirect method, 114-117

Joint width, 51
Junctions, 51

Landscape, 19
Laying mosaic, 49-52
joint width, 51
junctions, 51
small pieces, 51
Library shower, 20
Line, 12
Linear effects, 13

Marble, 131
riven, 63
Marble and smalti
garden mosaic, 34
Marble garden table,
44, 45
Materials, 9, 130-135
Mazzini, 97
Mesh, sticking to, 118-121
Methods
casting, 122-125
direct, 112, 113
indirect, 114-117
3-D objects, sticking
to, 126, 127
mesh, sticking to,
118-121
Mirrors
ceramic, 32, 33
circular, 84
slate, 72
square, 84
ungrouted glass, 68, 69
Mosaic
ancient art of, 6
angles, 51
backgrounds, 52
Christian, 7, 8
classical, 6, 7
faces and figures in,
87-97

haphazardly laid, 39
historical, 99-109
image, copying, 100
laying, 49-52
medium of, 12
modern, 8
textural, 65
ungrouted, 26
Moth table, 47

Offset, 52
Opus vermiculatum, 52
Outlining, 52

Pangolin, 55
Pattern, 12, 13
background, 76, 77
borders, 82, 83
foreground, 76
image, building up, 75
point of focus, as, 76
using, 76, 77
Paving slabs, 85
Perspective, 13, 16
Pigs, 61
Pisces, 60
Plaster and
plasterboard, 134
Porcupine, 54
Potato cod and
barracuda, 20

Rhinoceros, 56, 57
Road, The, 108
Road to Damascus, 72
Roman floor mosaics, 100
Roman Head, 109

San Vitale mosaic,
98-101, 104-107
Sand and cement, 133
screeds and renders, 134
Shapes, 12, 38, 39
Silicone, 132
Silver tiles, 131
Slate mirror, 72
Smalti, 34, 35, 131
Smalti and marble
panel, 66, 67

Square and circular
mirrors, 84
Streaks, 52
Stylization, 11-19
Summer mosaic, 19
Sunflower table, 61
Surface finish
influence of, 63
reflective mosaics, 64
textural mosaics, 65
Swirl table, 47

Tabletops
ceramic, 80, 81
crockery, 16, 17
fish, 58, 59
glazed ceramic, 30, 31
glazed tile, 40, 41
marble garden, 44, 45
moth, 47
sunflower, 61
swirl, 47
tartan, 78, 79
Tartan tabletop, 78, 79
Techniques, 9, 112-127
Terracotta, 134
Tile-backer board, 134
Tile cutters, 128
Tile nippers, 128
Tiler's sponge, 129
Timber, 134
Tools, 9, 128, 129
Trowels, 129
Tweezers, 129
Two figures, 96

Unglazed ceramic, 130
Ungrouted glass mirror,
68, 69

Virgo, 109
Vitreous glass, 130

Water beast, 102, 103
Waves, 52

Yellow tablecloth, 92, 93

Zogu, 96